The Origin of Humanness in the Biology of Love

Humberto Maturana Romesin
and Gerda Verden-Zöller

Edited by Pille Bunnell

imprint-academic.com

Copyright © Humberto Maturana Romesin, 2008

The moral rights of the author have been asserted.
No part of this publication may be reproduced in any form
without permission, except for the quotation of brief passages
in criticism and discussion.

Published in the UK by
Imprint Academic, PO Box 200, Exeter EX5 5YX, UK

Published in the USA by
Imprint Academic, Philosophy Documentation Center
PO Box 7147, Charlottesville, VA 22906-7147, USA

ISBN: 978184540 088 0

A CIP catalogue record for this book is available from the
British Library and US Library of Congress

Contents

Foreword by Pille Bunnell v
Poem xxii
Preface by Humberto Maturana Romesín 1
General Reflection 9
1. Prologue 11
2. Fundaments 14
3. Human Origins 48
4. Our Present 84
5. Overview 141

Appendices

1. Scientific Explanations 147
2. Structural Determinism & Structural Intersections . . 158
3. Systemic versus Genetic Determination 174
4. Virtual Realities and the Nervous System 189
5. Virtual Realities and Human Existence 197
6. Systemic/Analogical vs Local/Causal Reasoning . . . 204
7. Reality 209
8. Biology of Trust 214
9. Symbolization and Reality 216
10. Dimensions in Love 223
    References 228

Editor's Foreword

The Origin of Humanness in The Biology of Love

A path of changes

When Dr. Humberto Maturana handed me the manuscript for this book at the first American Society for Cybernetics Conference I attended in 1995, I had no idea that this would lead to a substantial change in my own life and career.

As a systems ecologist, I had known of his work, and had even attended a seminar he presented in my home town the year prior, but I had not then understood the depth of the work and its substantive implications for how we think about ourselves and all our relations—both in our cultural matrix and in the biosphere. It's not that the seminar had not been meaningful. In the 1994 Vancouver seminar, Maturana had spoken about the shift in the lives of children as they moved from the matristic ambience of a home culture to the ambience of a more patriarchal "real world" culture. As a result of the reflections this stimulated, my husband and I were willing to accept our then teenaged son's choice of an alternative school—a choice that all three of us look back on with gratitude.

Of course Dr. Maturana knew nothing of this as he handed me the manuscript. He was passing out copies, and I imagine he was hoping that someone would make a suggestion for where this little book could be published.

I was naïve enough to offer to edit the work. I did not realize how presumptuous I was, and how gracious he was in being willing to consider my offer. Nor did I realize that this would become a lengthy process that would afford me the enormous privilege of what amounted to personal tutoring from a foundational scholar of cybernetics. And I did not even dream how deeply these ideas would affect me, to the extent that I changed my career from a successful international environmental consultant to a university professor. I now love to teach, to inspire, and to expand the vision of students who in turn consistently find the material deeply and abidingly inspiring for how they live, both personally and professionally.

Once we began editing, Maturana generously and impeccably answered many emails, and sat with me, reviewing my proposed edits, during the breaks in several further conferences. I had secured a publishing agreement and the publisher waited patiently for the completion of the manuscript. Eventually both of us were content with the accuracy and the readability of the book. At that point, however, various extenuating circumstances intervened, and publication of the book was curtailed. Fortunately, the original edited manuscript has now been resurrected and we are all happy to present this book to a readership who may find it as seminal as I did.

Significance of Maturana's work

Now I would like to say a few words about why I find Maturana's body of work so important, and also why it is sometimes seen as difficult. My students have variously called it "chewy," "mental calisthenics," and "practical philosophy."

If I were to claim that any of the following is either true, or an interpretation of Maturana's work, then I would be acting inconsistently with the understanding that I have gained from it. All I can do, and all I wish to do, is offer my own understanding based on my own experience. I have found the work illuminating, compelling, and evocative of a manner of social and ecological living that I find vital, attractive and deeply resonant.

I write with the desire that what I say may trigger some insight or illumination in others. I cannot know — I am constitutionally not competent to know – what understanding or action now will later result in a world that we, as *Homo sapiens amans*, would like to have lived forth, along with all our relations, human and other. I do not know what words and actions lived now will have the eventual result that we, or our children, will not later live in regret. Yet, yet—I do think and believe that a manner of thinking that conserves reflection as well as love has the highest probability of becoming a world that we can live in through conserving our lineage as described by Maturana and Verden Zöller in this book. So this is what I want to speak of here—namely why I think Maturana's work leads to conserving reflection as a manner of thinking (as does the work of his colleagues, and of the many people around the world who have been inspired by it).

A network of ideas

I have noted over the years that different people find different entry points into the network of ideas, insights and explanations that constitute the lifework of Dr. Maturana. The different entry points[1] lead to different emphases. The original work was clearly in the domain of biology; and many people refer to Maturana's contribution of *autopoiesis*[2] as the central aspect, with further attention on structural coupling and *lineaging* (which they may consider equivalent to *evolution*). Others are enchanted by the experimental work on the nervous system, which leads to thinking about cognition and to our inability to claim any sort of privileged access to "reality." These people often refer to the body of

---

[1] I have noted entry points, but these are not the same as motives, though motives may influence which entry points appeal. As indicated in the logo of the institute formed around Maturana's work, namely Instituto Matriztico, people are usually interested in this work either due to curiosity or pain; or both. In my own case my curiosity was that of a scientist, and my pain was the angst I feel about the course of human activities on earth.

[2] For a brief explanation of Autopoiesis as the organization and realization of living systems, see Appendix 2. A more detailed treatment is found in Maturana, H. R. (2003). Autopoiesis, structural coupling and cognition: A history of these and other notions in the biology of cognition. *Cybernetics & Human Knowing*, 9(3-4), 5-34.

work as the Biology of Cognition. Yet others are more deeply taken by the relational dynamics of *emotioning* and *languaging*, and the consequent cultural implications, and see the whole as the Biology of Love. This book emphasizes the Biology of Love, as is evident in its title. There are also people who approach the work from a philosophical interest, and are concerned with ontological and epistemological implications.

In my view all of these are encompassed in what Maturana and his colleagues now call the Biological and Cultural Matrix of Human Existence. For ease of introducing it to students, I refer to it as a network of ideas, insights, and explanations. I also tell my students that this is a peculiar network. Let's say the letters of the alphabet represent the various concepts and ideas where they have to learn A before they can understand B, but they cannot really understand A fully until they have learned B. The same is true for C, D, E and F; each of which contributes more depth to A, and to B, as well as to each other (*Figure 1*, opposite page).

Figure 1. A Network of Explanations

This drawing is not intended to describe the whole matrix of ideas encompassed by Maturana's work, nor that of his colleagues at Instituto Matriztico. Indeed, some of the ideas included here may differ from what they include or emphasize. I show my figure here partly to give a sense of the breadth of ideas involved, but mostly to emphasize the network nature of the whole. All the lines in this figure imply reciprocity in understanding. Not all connections are shown; my purpose here is to suggest a density of connections among the ideas — which thus constitute a coherent whole.

(A similar type of figure was presented in Maturana and Varela's *The Tree of Knowledge*, and mine is not intended as a replacement for that).

closed nervous system
sensory motor coordination

mistake, illusion & experience

cognition
knowing, understanding
expansion of relational domains
linear and systemic rationality
intelligence

systemic dynamics
spontaneous constitution
causality
contextual inertia
conservation and change
structural intersection
dynamic temporal architecture

systems
simple, complex unities
boundary
structure, organization
structural determinism
cycles, feedback
recurrence, iteration
recursion

(objectivity)
explanations
generative mechanisms
prediction
changing the question
being and doing
Reality and multiverse

living systems
autopoiesis
behavior & adaptation
constitutive domains
ontogeny

epigenesis

evolution
structural coupling
environment, niche
plasticity & selection
biosphere
natural drift

emotioning
relational domains
discrimination & preference
love, fear, anger
mien & consequence

languaging
consensuality
objects
naming & distinctions
observer & observing
stories & causality
reflection
self consciousness

premises
energy
matter
mathematics
time

human origins
historical explanations
neoteny, intimacy, pleasure
conservation by children
expansion as lineage

culture
evolution of culture
cultural inertia
conversation
lineages of language
matriztic & patriarchal

concerns
responsibility
autonomy, freedom
ethical behaviour
soul, spirituality & intimacy
mystery, beauty
sustainability
wisdom

Thus it is a coherent network that deepens as one engages with it. However one has to begin somewhere, so I propose that we begin with the concept represented by the letter A (which varies according to the interest of the group being addressed). I caution them that since they know that A will appear different after learning B, they have to approach the whole with the willingness to not assume that any element is complete in isolation from the rest. One has to be willing to let go of what one knows about any aspect at any moment in order to understand it, and the whole, more fully. The process of becoming an expert in any field relies on a similar approach.

None of this means that the iInsights one first gains from A, or from A plus B, are invalid; it just means that the implications and applicability deepen as the insights themselves become both epigenic[3] and reciprocally illuminating. Such is, after all, the natural course of learning; even if we often think it is simply cumulative — with the unfortunate consequence that often our educational system tends to reduce understanding to knowledge and knowledge to collections of facts.

Of course many elements contained in this network of ideas have been explored by others before; Maturana himself has often claimed that there is nothing new in what he says. However if readers or listeners stop their own engagement with "Ah, yes, that is what so and so said" — then their understanding is limited by what they knew before. Perhaps what is new is the re-invention of these elements as a whole network of understanding in the modern context of science and humanities. In the long run, authorship is rather less relevant than the consequences of *living* an understanding. It is in the relational domain where the acknowledgement of contribution or inspiration, from any source, is a manner of living in love and respect.

---

[3] Epigenic is a word that originally derives from embryology; where each new development can only take place on the ground of the previous development. This applies generally to many processes, and particularly to learning.

Domains

In writing this foreword I had thought to highlight several key themes. I find myself immediately caught in the network; unable to leave out A or B or E or F, as they are all relevant to the whole. So instead I will address an aspect that I have been thinking about lately; namely domains. Though domains and their implications are in the foreground of my thoughts now, I am aware that I too will think differently some time later. Understanding always follows an epigenic path, so that one is always where one is, where the current ideas rest on what preceded and act as the ground for whatever may yet arise.

In a recent article[4] Maturana shows how cultural inventions such as time are natural outcomes of our living together. These inventions do not cause us problems as long as we accept the operational coherences relevant to the structural domain to which our actions pertain, and as long as we do not confuse domains.

Domains are easily confused because we are generally not aware of them. In one respect they do not even exist, as they represent a slice, or perspective of an imaginary n-dimensional matrix, and the making of the slice is an act of simplification that enables local action. In another view, we live always in one domain or other. We are never present, or acting, in the whole of the imaginary n-dimensional matrix. Each domain is complete in itself, and only partial if we imagine a whole in which they all exist. Yet each is different in its internal coherence, its relevance, and its possibilities. We, like other animals, flow easily from domain to domain in the course of our daily living. Unlike other animals, we do this emphatically also in language, and in language it causes us problems because we often operate under the implicit assumption that all that we speak and all that we know exists in a single domain called "reality." When we cannot co-opt our perceptions, ideas, or experi-

---

[4] Time as an Imaginary Spatial Dimension, *Cybernetics and Human Knowing* Vol 15. No. 2

ences into this supposedly singular domain, we often consider them delusions or aberrations of one kind or another.

As Maturana has said every distinction reveals some regularity in our living, and obscures others. As each distinction also brings forth the domain in which it is valid, each domain also reveals some regularity in our living and obscures others.

We do not live in a "flatworld" of one domain, or one collection of regularities. We shift planes, dimensions, or domains in the flow of our activities and relationships, and the flow of emotioning and languaging is commensurate with this flow. Our pedestrian rules of logic are valid within any given domain, but become problematic if we shift domains, as we may easily do without noting it, even in the middle of the argument. Logical constructs only work properly as long as we are careful that we do not cross domains. Paradoxes arise when we do not pay attention to changes in domain.

I began to notice this prior to encountering Maturana's work as I noticed what I considered careless logic in the figures that people drew to explain various systems dynamics. Now, one of Maturana's seminal figures serves as a referent for my own vision and for my teaching. Maturana's figure (Figure 2) is iconic, and I think evocative. The circular arrow represents a living system in recursive autopoiesis, (its constitutive domain, or physiology). The living system as a whole also has a reciprocal adaptive relationship with its niche (its relational domain or behaviour). I find it easy to explain that a living system cannot persist as such without conserving both. Yet we cannot claim that one causes the other, nor can we explain either in terms of the other, even though what takes place in one does alter the dynamics of the other.

Pedagogically this figure serves as a touchstone for noting the difference between the generative domain and the phenomenal domain — and for recognizing that confusing these looks leads to troublesome misunderstandings.

Inasmuch as domains are sets, or networks of relevant regularities, they can be distinguished according to various

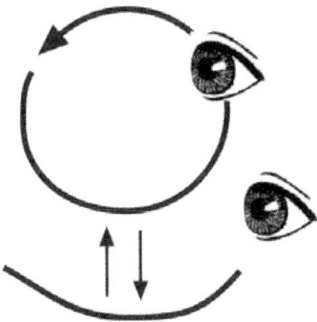

Figure 2. Two different looks of an observer in noting either the generative domain (top eye), or the resultant phenomenon in a different domain (lower eye). This figure is Maturana's iconic representation of a living system that remains conserved as such as long as both autopoiesis and adaptation persist.

different looks, as these arise with different interests, contexts, or concerns. Thus we can name the kind of concern that appears to prevail, and we can speak of operational domains, generative domains, relational domains, and more. If someone wants to analyze domains as if they had an existence other than in either action or in reflection, this can lead to confusion. Relational domains, which Maturana equates to emotions, are thus distinguished through different constellations of possible actions as one lives a particular local regularity. Again, we shift domains fluidly, so we flow easily from one relational domain or emotion to another (hence *emotioning*), and if we pause to reflect we see that the internal coherence, or logic, of these differs. We think and act differently in different relational domains.

Like other domains, relational domains cannot thus be collapsed one into another. However, we can navigate from one to another such that the social consequence is harmonious. Sometimes this becomes a delicate matter as we find ourselves engaged in multiple incommensurate relational domains. When this happens we sometimes simply isolate our presence in one from our presence in another. Indeed it is socially not only acceptable, but "proper" to keep our emotional family lives separate from the emotions in our working relations. At other times we cannot fully isolate our relational domains, and we either find a path of behaviour that is acceptable in all, or some of the relational domains change or even collapse. I think we feel best when we don't experience a sense of dissonance as we move from one emotion to another, as we do remember at least our actions, if not how we ourselves were when we were different. This is of course easiest if one retains the overarching emotion of love, as the basic constituent of our humanness — as is described in this book.

Writing from within the matrix

One further point I would like to address is the complaint sometimes heard that Maturana's writing is difficult to read. Of course part of the difficulty is that each element is part of a matrix, or network of ideas. It isn't linear, and thus it requires a manner of thinking that differs from our cultural habits. Though there may be other reasons for the perceived difficulty, I want to address here the notion of circularity in writing.

Maturana has found that editors sometimes try to clarify his work through removing what they see as repetition or redundancy. In many cases what they are doing is removing the circularities. Circularities are important because they launch and sustain a generative process. The understanding that they are intended to evoke arises only through the operation of the circularity.

All circularities, whether they consist of iterations (the process is reapplied to the result of the process) or recursions (the process is applied to itself) operate like this. The phenomenon, whether it is considered tangible or psychic, only lasts as long as the generative process continues to operate. This isn't easily apparent to us given that we can name the phenomenon, and then use that name as if it replaced the phenomenon. What happens is that the same word can either evoke the generative process which gives rise to the phenomenon (and it does this quite rapidly as one becomes expert in that particular circularity), or it can be "flattened" into an object that is used in another domain of coordinations. The same word that signifies or triggers a generative cognitive operation can also persist as an object that coordinates behaviour in an entirely different operational domain.

It is not always easy to note whether a word is being treated as a generative process or an object, even when one realizes that these differences exist. And it is very difficult to realize that one needs to operate mental circularities for the phenomenon of meaning inherent in those to arise if one expects only descriptions and definitions. Since Maturana's writing and thinking include many circular, generative processes, this may render understanding difficult until one perceives that circularities need to be operated (sometimes through several cycles) in order for the whole to be understood.

The second point I wish to address is the style and apparent intent of some of the writing. I have asked Maturana why he writes as he does, and he has answered that he wants to be understood. Someone trained in writing for a broad public would find this claim almost incredible, as that form of training emphasizes representing ideas in terms that the readership already understands. The writing has to be different when one wants to evoke the arising of new understanding, and wants to do so in a manner that will not be misunderstood.

Metaphorical explanations are easy to read, as are stories that exemplify a particular idea. The problem with this kind of writing is that the direction is largely set by the prior knowledge of the listener. Metaphors and stories are constitutively open to being understood very differently by each listener. However, if someone wishes to understand what the speaker or writer intends, or the speaker or writer wants to be understood in the terms that he or she specifies, a different kind of writing or speaking is required.

In speaking, in personal presence, the listener can be enchanted to follow a path of explanations, stories, and evocations such that the understanding results. Many people have told me that once they have heard Maturana speak, they can then read his writing with much greater ease. They have learned how to think along the paths he evokes in the multifaceted, consensual dance that personal presence allows. In writing, however, evoking a new understanding is more difficult as there is no opportunity for the writer to respond to the flow of the reader. Hence when a writer wishes to be unambiguous, he or she has to provide an unambiguous operational process for understanding what is written. With this sort of writing the reading is slow, and one may have to read a sentence several times to obtain the resultant understanding.

That said, I think Maturana presents his views here in an easy flow. More technical or more demanding bits have been moved to the appendices.

Conserving the impetus to reflect

Early in the initial editing process I told Maturana that I thought his work was a cosmology. He was quiet for a moment, then asked me what I meant by *cosmology*. When I answered that a cosmology was a coherent way of understanding and explaining all of one's experiences, he conceded that he also had tried to use that word but had found it evoked the wrong sort of listening. Within my meaning of the word, we all live in a cosmology, creating our cosmos in a way that is congruent with the culture in which we find ourselves, and with our individual life experiences. I do not have a word that better expresses "everything" than the word *cosmos*, so for the next few paragraphs I ask the reader to temporarily accept my meaning of cosmology which to me feels more encompassing than *world view*.

When I was first learning this material, there was a point when I felt as if I were on a magic flying carpet from which I could perceive everything. It was heady, exhilarating. Then one day I noticed that in fact there was no carpet. I was alone in "mid air." Yet; I did not crash and fall, nor was I isolated. Instead I found myself comfortable in a newly sensed radical responsibility. This did not appear to me as a burden, but rather as a sense of delicious autonomy that came with a comfortable ethical care for how I engaged with the world. Of course I have since committed many mistakes, that is, I have acted in ways that in retrospect were not the best way of navigating some delicate matter. What I have found myself conserving is a willingness to engage in reflection, of seeing and changing that is not dependent on any thing or any idea.

An individual always grows in a culture in a manner that is in part determined by that culture. Basic premises regarding existence, relevance and even how to think, are acquired prior to having developed the capacity in language to reflect, or to experience self consciousness.[5] The individual accepts and lives according to a cosmology implicit in these premises and thus acts in a fashion that is coherent with that understanding. This in turn constitutes the cultural matrix, which then validates that understanding and is conserved as the cultural context for new individuals. Thus a cosmology is usually conserved in a culture through an intergenerational circularity (Figure 3 A). In this situation culture and cosmology appear as one and the same, though they occur in different domains. I take a culture to comprise a network of activities and relationships among a group of people, it cannot be encompassed in a single individual. A cosmology (as I am using the word here), on the other hand, pertains to an individual – though of course it can be abstracted and described as typical of a culture.

The difference between most cosmologies and what I have come to understand from Maturana's work comes through the inclusion of a second kind of circularity within the culture-individual circularity. Here, the cosmology is applied to the cosmology; that is the process is applied to itself, which makes it recursive. In order for this to be possible, the process of reflection is required; and reflection takes

---

[5] Maturana, H. 2006. Self Consciousness: How? When? Where? *Constructivist Foundations*, Volume 1, No. 3.

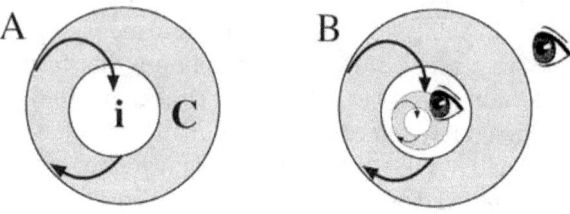

Figure 3. Conservation of cosmologies in cultures. The individual (i) is the small white circle and the culture in which s/he lives is the large grey circle (C). A represents the general case, and B represent the addition of a recursive reflection as an element of the cosmology.

place in the locus where a cosmology exists as such, that is within an individual. Reflection implies the ability to release what one believes or thinks, and to metaphorically step outside of that to consider it (external eye, Figure 3 B). Of course one immediately sees that one is not really outside, so one sees oneself both as reflecting on the cosmology, and as the individual who reflects on the cosmology, embedded in the culture (inner eye, Figure 3 B). This double look has a peculiar effect that I, and others, experience as an emancipation, a sense of freedom, or a psychic mobility.

Though any particular reflection easily collapses into a description or observation, the function of reflection itself remains, so it regenerates itself. There is thus the possibility of an endless progress of reflections, each one grounded on whatever preceded it. Indeed I find it difficult to experientially retain an awareness of reflection as a process beyond one recursion, namely the "reflection of reflection." If I try to mentally actually make further recursions, it becomes an abstraction that describes the process, as in Figure 4. Yet the description may be enough to engender in us an intuitive grasp of how reflection is conserved, and may evoke a new reflection on reflection, or a reflection on the process of recursive reflection.

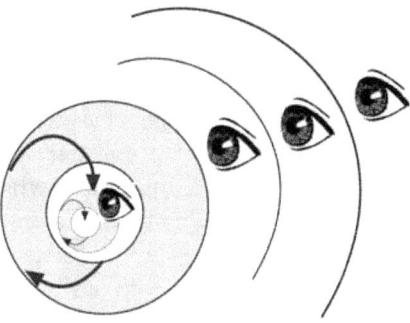

Figure 4. An endless progress of reflection, as enabled by the recursion on reflection.

For a cosmology to be recursive, it must conserve reflection, and for it to conserve reflection, the process of reflection must be inherent in the cosmology. This is made possible by a significant aspect of Maturana's cosmology; namely he has impeccably avoided grounding his network of explanations in any externality, including those that are difficult to refute because they are invisible or taboo. If there were an externality, one would not be able to "get outside" that externality, and thus the application of the cosmology to itself could not take place. In this cosmology there is no referent other than the happening of the process of human living, with all that we do and experience as we live and reflect on ourselves, our doings, and our world.

Implications of conserving reflection

The consequence of reflection cannot be predetermined. Thus as reflection is conserved, a culture will change along a path of changes that cannot be predetermined. This may concern anyone who wishes to retain or be loyal to a particular idea, belief, or even moral code. It is only really comfortable to contemplate the matter of openness in cultural change if one accepts that humans have evolved as loving animals, as described in this book. Of course we could further evolve to become *Homo sapiens aggressans*[6], or *Homo sapiens arrogans*, but at this time, most of the people I have encountered indicate that they feel well when acting as *Homo sapiens amans*. Furthermore, and again in my experience, a propensity to act as *H.s. amans* shows up when reflection begins; as indeed is inherent in many practices that encourage people to "stop and think about what you really want." Hence I believe that this biological constitution is still fundamental in us humans, and that reflection appears to enable us to act in accordance with our biological constitution. I think this is part of the sense of emancipation I referred to earlier.

Without the ability to reflect on all the premises inherent in one's cosmology, one is constrained to acting only within the constraints of an inherited, usually implicit cosmology. Though the specific consequence of an open-ended cultural drift cannot be determined, I can trust that a drift which conserves wisdom (*sapiens*) and love (*amans*) will result in a world that I would like to imagine for our children and for the earth. I believe that a change in culture that arises along a path of reflections is far more likely to lead to humans becoming a sustainable species than the conservation of currently prevailing cultures and cosmologies.

In conclusion I claim that the network of ideas, insights and explanations of Maturana's cosmology conserves an opening for reflection that allows an escape whenever the answers to the deep questions about humanity and life

---

[6] My original suggestion in 1995 had been **Homo sapiens amans** for the species and subspecies, with the subspecies **H.s. aggressans** and **H.s. arrogans**. Maturana has just reviewed a draft of this foreword and has offered what I think is an excellent refinement for this notion. He now speaks of **Homo sapiens-amans amans** as the original form, where the hyphenated **sapiens-amans** refers to the arising of languaging under the emotioning of love in the original small family group. The second **amans** refers to the manner of living since then, which means that further subspecies would take the form of **Homo sapiens-amans aggressans** and **Homo sapiens-amans arrogans**. This makes it clear that we claim that our basic fundament remains **sapiens-amans**, the "wise-loving" hominid, and the other manners of being are variations on top of that.

become treated as if true and rigid. Dr. Humberto Maturana Romesin, I thank you most deeply for all that you have contributed. I hope that the readers of this book will experience the pleasure of insight and the delight in reflection that I have had in following this path.

Pille Bunnell
Vancouver, BC, October 2008

Humanness

Now ... what makes humanness?
Languaging.
What makes a man a man?
Nothing more than his sex.
But ... what makes a man a human being?
His sensuality and tenderness in
open awareness of his earthly
interconnections as he dances the
recursive dance of eating
playing, and kissing.
And ... what makes a woman a woman?
The same
through her own sexuality.
But ... what makes her a human being?
Her tenderness and sensuality in
open awareness of her earthly
interconnectedness as she dances
the recursive dance of eating,
playing, and kissing.

What is the difference, then?
None and everything, since the
woman is always aware of being
in her humanness a cosmic source
out of nothingness, while the man
has to learn this anew when he
becomes seduced and enchained by
the delight of linear reasoning that
the woman has always known to be
a transitory winter blossom.

And novelty, what is novelty in all this?
An unexpected turn in an always
recursive dancing dance.
Empty seems human life to be!
Yes! ... Or rich, in the fullness
of an always changing present
of eating, playing, and kissing.

Humberto Maturana

Preface
Origin of Humanness

This book arose in the crossing of two paths of research and reflection in relation to the origin of humanness. The first of these was my intent to visualize and understand the evolutionary origin of humanness, and the other, that of Dr. Gerda Verden-Zöller, was her attempt to show observationally the arising of self-consciousness in the child in the early mother–child play relations. Although this book was written in 1994–96, I think that its contents are still valid now, some fifteen years later.

In my approach to the theme of evolution I had developed some unorthodox notions about the actual mechanism that drives the process of evolution that I shall summarize in the following statements (see Maturana and Mpdozis, 2000):

- The actual mechanism that drives evolution is structural drift in the conservation of both living and adaptation in the present, in an independent and continuously newly arising changing medium, not the selection of those best adapted to a preexisting medium.
- Natural selection is a consequence of natural drift, not the generative mechanism of evolution. The generative mechanism of evolution is natural drift.
- Living systems occur as discrete organisms in the medium that makes them possible.
- Adaptation is not a variable; adaptation is a relation of operational congruence between the changing organism and the changing medium in which it lives.
- If the relation of adaptation is lost, the organism dies. So an organism either slides in the medium in the path in which its living is conserved, or it dies (disintegrates).

- What is conserved in the constitution of a lineage through reproduction is adaptation, namely, the organism-niche relation in which its manner of living is realized and conserved.

- A lineage of organisms arises when a particular dynamic organism-niche relation begins to be conserved as a manner of living from one generation to the next through systemic reproduction.

- Systemic reproduction occurs as both the organization of the reproducing organism and the configuration of the medium in which it realizes its living are conserved together as a simple result of the conservation of the realization of that manner of living by the offspring of that organism. This occurs in the interplay of genetics and the behavioral preferences that guide the living of the organism in its niche. When this happens, the manner of living conserved from one generation to the next, as a particular configuration of organism-niche relations, becomes the operational dynamic center around which everything else is open to change; thus defining the class identity of the lineage through its systemic conservation.

- A lineage lasts as long as the dynamic configuration of organism-niche relation that constitutes the manner of living and defines its class identity of an organism is conserved through systemic reproduction.

- The evolutionary path that a lineage follows is the path of structural drift in which the organism-niche relation that defines it is conserved. So, if we wish to understand the origin and history of a lineage we must find the initial manner of living that began to be conserved as an organism-niche relation and the variations of that manner of living conserved as part of it in its natural drift, so that the members of that lineage live now as they live now.

- The present manner of living of the members of a lineage is the result of a history of natural drift, not an attainment of progressive improvement of its adaptation to a pre-existing medium.

Under this manner of thinking, if I wanted to see how humanness arose and has become what it is now, I had to answer the question "What manner of living (organism-niche relation) began to be conserved in our ancestors so that we live now as we live now?" These were my central reflections when I met Dr. Verden-Zöller.

What Dr. Verden-Zöller basically wanted to understand was the arising of self-consciousness in the child; and she thought that this took place in the early childhood of each child in the course of his or her intimate relation with his or her mother. Accordingly she thought that the place to research this question was during the early mother–child play relations, and she turned to study those relations in relatively isolated communities in West Germany after the war. Here I summarize in my words what I thought were her basic findings at the time we met:

- The main task in the growing child is learning his or her body, and he or she does so in the intimate and playful close contact with his or her mother.
- The worlds that the child lives arise in the mother–child relation as the child does together with his or her mother whatever they do together.
- It is in the mother–child play that the baby creates his or her self-distinctions. And he or she does so as a matter of course in the flow of his or her play in intimate body contact with his or her mother as they touch each other reciprocally, and in their handling and touching whatever they manipulate and distinguish together.
- The playfulness of the child in his or her mother–child relation becomes the operational-relational fundament for the different worlds that he or she generates along his or her whole life.

Listening to her and reflecting on her findings I became aware that she had the answer to my question. Indeed, I realized that it was the organism-niche relation defined by the conservation of the emotioning of the mother–child relations of play, as well as of variations in the manner of living around it, that guided the evolutionary course of our primate ancestors. This happened in a coexistence centered in love thus generating an ambiance in which living in languaging could arise as the manner of living whose conservation from one generation to the next in the learning of the children, constituted humanness as the basic loving manner of living that we live now. While we talked about this I wrote this little book as a daring proposition of what we thought must have been the evolutionary history of our lineage; namely, through the systemic conservation generation after generation of a manner of living in the learning of the children, and not through some fortunate series of mutations and genetic recombinations.

The conservation of a manner of living from one generation to the next in the learning and habits of the offspring of the members of a lineage through systemic reproduction both guides and co-opts all genetic variations that facilitate or realize that manner of living as an organism-niche operational-relational whole. I still consider now that this vision of the nature of the evolutionary process is valid.

When this little book was written, more that ten years ago, these ideas about evolution were not acceptable. The idea that the reproduction was a systemic process that involved the niche as well as the operational present state of the genetic system of the reproductive cells of the reproducing organism operating as an integrated whole was not easy to understand and accept. Since then biological understanding has developed and we now know that as reproduction takes place the new organism is formed in the fusion or division of active operating cells that carry with them their present state of living in the form of the network of nuclear and cytoplasmic processes that realize them in that moment of their living. Furthermore, we are now fully aware of the fact that that network of nuclear and cytoplasmic process involves all active and inactive genes as well as all the different molecules that constitute the dynamic molecular architecture of the realization of their present particular form of autopoiesis. Moreover, we biologists are also aware now that the initial systemic conditions that arise in the process of reproduction constitute only the starting point of the individual epigenetic history of the new organism, and that this epigenetic history will go one way or another according to which are the relational circumstances in which the organism realizes-conserves its autopoiesis in its organism-niche relation.

Therefore, although what we write in this little book appeared to be a daring evolutionary proposition in 1994, it now seems more than plausible. When Lamark and Darwin were in their different historical moments attempting to explain adaptation in the history of living system they thought of adaptation as a variable, and seeing the medium as a preexisting "container" to which the new organisms had to accommodate. Given this premise they felt that the happenings of the individual life histories had to have a presence in the life of their offspring. So, they proposed different approaches to the subject of adaptation suggesting different views of inheritance to make a historical connection between the successive generations. What they could not see then was that adaptation is necessarily a constant relation of operational coherence between the organism and its niche in the continuous realization of its living, and that both organism and niche spontaneously change together congruently.

After writing this little book, I turned my reflections to see the implications of the understanding of what we say in it, but I was not fully clear about how to connect love with our present manner of living. I thought that love was the most fundamental emotion in all aspects of our life, but I did not know how to reveal how love operated in our daily living until in the course of a conversation, my colleague Ximena Dávila Yáñez said to me the following: "Humberto, I have made a discovery, I have realized that the pain or suffering for which a person asks for help in the relational domain is always of cultural origin, and I have also realized that such pain arises as an experience of negation of love that the person that lives it accepts somehow as something that is culturally legitimate". And she added: "Furthermore, the person that consults me also tells me without being aware that he or she is doing so, where in the relational-operational matrix of her living occurred the negation of love as well as the path to come out of the self-devaluation that he or she is conserving in all aspects of her daily living since then".

When I asked Ximena what she did when the consulting person asked her for relational help, as I listened to her I realized through her answer that she did what I had not been able to do. I used to say that love was the first medicine, and when I was asked, *how does love operate, and what to do to love?* I answered saying, *"just love, it is easy, love operates in the act of loving"*, but nobody seemed to be able see the act of loving or how the act of loving was done. Ximena Dávila, however, with her answer was showing to me that she knew what to do as she put into action her understanding of the interplay of the biology of cognition and the biology of love in a reflective conversation with the result that the persons who consulted her recovered self-love and self-respect, and felt liberated of their pain and suffering. Later she developed the notion of *cultural-biology* to refer to the intrinsic biological-cultural nature of humanness that she was showing in her work of reflexive conversations with the persons that consulted her, and which we now call the *biological-cultural matrix of human existence*.

The different worlds that we human beings generate in our biological-cultural existence occur as different networks of conversations in the form of different networks of coordinations of coordinations of doings and emotioning in the realization of our living. Furthermore, these networks of conversations happen as different dynamics of the molecular architecture of the organism-niche relation that is the realization of the living of any organism which adopt in us the particular form of the organism-niche relation of our living in the biological-cultural matrix of our human existence.

The notion of cultural-biology proposed by Ximena brings forth a vision of the dynamic architecture of the biological-cultural nature of humanness that usually remains beyond our understanding hidden in the semantic notions that we use to talk about the different realities that we generate in our living. In other words, what the understanding of the biological-cultural nature of our humanness brings to us, and specially has given to me, is a more expanded fundamental vision of the different realities that we human beings may live. In particular, it has shown to me the nature of our emotional daily living and of the biological-cultural fundaments of our always present intimate desire for a daily living in which we realize and conserve honesty and, therefore, ethics.

Living beings occur as dynamic molecular entities that operate as totalities in a relational space, and they are realized as different kinds of organisms through the conservation of different organism-niche relations as different manners of living. Thus, we human beings exist in the conservation of an organism-niche relation which as a manner of living occurs in a relational space transcending the molecular dynamics that make it possible. And we human beings do so in the unity of body and mind through the integration of our emotions and our doings as we live our existence of loving languaging relational-reflective beings, conscious of the nature of our humanness in the deep desire of an ethical coexistence.

In the course of our conversations we decided to create a place where we would do research in the domain of humanness, and we created the Matriztic Institute in the year 2000 as a place to work and do research in the domain of the art and science of constitutive ontological thinking and doing. Now the Matriztic Institute is the place where I do all my work while following this path.

Finally, I would like to thank Dr. Pille Bunnell for the interest and appreciation that she showed for the contents of this little book when I presented it to her after my unsuccessful attempts to publish it some time in the years 1994 to 1996. And I wish to thank her for the interesting conversations that we had about the book, for her care in editing this work, and for her suggestion that I could use the expression *amans* in the denomination of our lineage to emphasize what I said as I claimed that love was the fundamental emotion that made possible the arising of languaging in the ancestral family.

Humberto Maturana Romesín
Instituto Matríztico
www.matriztica.org
July, 2008

General Reflection

This book presents a scientific, not a philosophical work. As a scientific work it entails speculations and explanations, as well as an unorthodox view about the mechanism that has guided the history of living systems. Our basic claim is that the history of living systems is one in which both living and variations in the manner of living have been conserved through the systemic reproduction of both the condition and manner of living as lineages of different kinds of living systems. All this will be explained in the course of the book; we mention it here only to invite the reader to read in a manner, which is open to see what we say. Once the reader has seen all the considerations which ground this claim, he or she may be inspired by our reflections or dismiss them, but in either case do so based on his or her understanding of what we say.

In this book we the authors reflect about the consequences of what we think, explain, and claim about human life, and we make ethical considerations about those consequences. Scientists frequently say that they are not responsible for the consequences of their findings, because consequences depend on how their findings are used. We think, however, that we scientists are ordinary human beings who have made science their professional manner of living, and thus what happens with their findings and explanations is also a matter that concerns them. Because of this we make ethical reflections throughout the book, reflections that are not part of our argument, but rather invite the reader to make his or her own reflections keeping in mind they are reflections, not scientific statements.

Finally, this book has two major parts. The first is our explanatory proposition of what must have happened for humanness to have arisen in the primate history to which we belong. This part contains our arguments, none of which falls outside the domain of biology, even if some of them are unorthodox. The second part is made up of a series of appendices that deal with different arguments in a deeper and more formal way than in the text of the first. This second part is conceived to be read interlaced with the first, but it can also be read independently.

Chapter 1
Prologue

We modern human beings frequently live in strife with each other, and suffer for it. War and peace seem to be basic polar elements of human relations, yet we are not happy in this manner of living in mutual negation; we dislike it. Moreover, in disliking this manner of living we become ill as individuals, or we think that humanity is ill and has been ill for a long time. In the midst of this unhappiness we discover, as we have discovered many times during the last five or six thousand years of our history that we have been living in blindness: about others, about nature, about justice, about collaboration. As we realize that we do not like this we invent, and have invented on many occasions, religious and political systems in which peace and love are to prevail, or humanistic philosophies and economic theories that are intended to save human beings from mutual exploitation and abuse.

Most of the time our efforts have failed, our humanizing paradigms have ended up being dehumanizing, and the religious and political systems that we invented with the intent of generating human wellbeing became sources of tyrannies. But we have always tried again. How does it come about that we try again? How is it that we fail and yet try again? How is it that we human beings have ethical concerns? How is it that we human beings care for each other, even though we live now, and have lived for the last five or six thousand years of our history in a manner wherein we frequently deny each other through competition, war, abuse, and mutual manipulation?

Our purpose in this essay is to answer these questions. Yet, in order to do so we want first to reformulate them in terms more akin to our immediate daily-life situations, because we think that they must be answered as features of daily life, which is where the conservation or loss of life takes place.

Clinicians say that a doctor begins to act in the moment in which he or she accepts a call for help, and indeed this happens. If a mother calls the doctor in anxiety because her child is ill, and the mother says, "Doctor, thank you for coming; I do not know what happened, but my child has gotten better since I spoke with you." How did that occur? What happened that the child became better when the doctor accepted the call, and would have become worse if the doctor had not? Doctors also say that the first medicine is the bed, and indeed, when the sick person is put to bed, he or she begins to improve. What happens? Is this improvement merely the result of a reduction of metabolism through repose?

We know as part of European history, that Rasputin, a wandering monk related to the court of the last Russian Czar, had a great curative influence on the young hemophilic Czarevitch. His influence was so great, that on one occasion, when the boy was bleeding after falling off a horse, his bleeding stopped when Rasputin answered the Czarina's request for help by sending her a telegram saying: "Do not worry, the child is out of danger and will get better, I come immediately". How could this cure have happened?

We modern human beings frequently use war in our attempts to solve human conflicts. How is it that war never solves human conflicts; at best it only changes the domain in which the conflicts take place, so that they are eventually solved through mutual respect? According to us the solution in mutual respect, when it happens, belongs to our ethical concern as a feature of the biology of love. The Declaration of Human Rights by the newly created United Nations after the end of the Second World War is a milestone in ethical concerns in modern human history. How is it that we had ethical concerns then? How is it that ethical concerns remain an important part of modern human life? Are they a product of our reason or of our emotions?

Experience—that which we distinguish as happening to us—cannot be denied. Daily life shows us that even though we live in war and hurt each other, we are loving animals that become bodily and psychically ill when deprived of love, and that love is both the first medicine and the fundament for the recovery of somatic and psychic health. We are love-dependent animals at all ages. Indeed, most if not all human suffering arises in the negation of love and is cured through the restoration of love. How can this be so? What happens in us through love?

Our purpose in this essay is to explain how it is that we are love dependent animals, and how we have come to live our present culture as if this were not so. We intend to do so by presenting our view of the origin of humanness in the biology of love. However, in order to attain this end, we begin by saying a few words about the biological and epistemological fundaments on which our proposition stands. We do so by speaking first about explanations, then about our biological history, and finally, about language and emotions. After that, we consider our human biological origin in the mother/child relation and sexual intimacy, and we end with some reflections about our cultural present and about what we can do.

Chapter 2

Fundaments

In this section we present the biological and epistemological fundaments on which our proposition stands. If the reader so wishes, he or she can go directly to the beginning of our proposition in Chapter 3, Human Origins, and return to this later as he or she thinks is desirable.

Explaining

In general terms, explanations are answers to questions that demand an explanation as an answer and which are accepted as such by a listener. In particular terms, an explanation is the proposition of a generative mechanism or process, such that that which the observer wants to explain arises as a result or consequence of its operation. This is why an explanation in any domain always has the form: "If this and this happens, then the result is such and such". Therefore, in an explanation, the observer deals with two nonintersecting phenomenal domains; namely, the phenomenal domain in which the generative mechanism takes place, and the phenomenal domain in which the explained phenomenon occurs. Explanations, accordingly, do not and cannot constitute phenomenal reductions; that is, as one explains, one does not reduce one phenomenal domain to another. When we explain we do not express the phenomenon or experience to be explained in more basic or more fundamental terms, as is frequently said; rather we propose a generative mechanism that gives rise to the phenomenon or experience to be explained in a different domain as a consequence of its operation.

We speak in daily life, or we speak as scientists, explicitly or implicitly saying that we explain phenomena, and that these phenomena are processes that take place independently of our doings in a domain external to us as observers, even if we somehow participate in them. However, we do not explain processes that occur external to us, and take place independent from our doings. We are always operating as observes, so that in fact what we explain is our experience—that which we as observers distinguish as directly or indirectly happening to us, or in us. So, from now on we shall speak of experiences, rather than phenomena, and if we speak of phenomena, we shall mean experiences. We see, we touch, we measure, and so forth, and in the same way that we use the coherences and regularities of our seeing, our touching, and our measuring as we formulate, describe, or present what we want to explain, we use the regularities and coherences of our seeing, touching, and measuring to propose the generative mechanism that will be our explanatory proposition. That is, we use our experiential coherences in one domain to propose an explanation of our experiential coherences in another domain. We always make an explanation by proposing a generative mechanism. A generative mechanism consists of a process, that if it were to take place, the result would be the experience to be explained. The experience to be explained takes place in a different experiential domain than the one in which the proposed generative mechanism takes place. Thus, we explain our experiences with our experiences, and regardless of which non-intersecting experiential domains the proposed generative mechanism and the experience to be explained take place, we always explain relying completely on the regularities of our experiences.

This is not all, however. For a generative mechanism that is proposed as an explanation—the formal aspect of any explanation—to be accepted as such, it must also satisfy some condition that the observer adds from his or her own choice, or preference, as he or she listens. This condition is the informal aspect of any explanation, and it can be anything at all. The informal aspect of an explanation may be implicit or explicit, and the listener may or may not be aware that he or she is adding something, but it is always present as the generative mechanism is accepted as an explanation.

The informal condition is what gives an explanation its character and defines its kind. As a result, there are as many different kinds of explanations as there are different kinds of informal conditions that can be added by the observer in his or her listening as he or she accepts a particular generative mechanism as an explanation. The informal aspect in the explanations that scientists accept is what we have called the criterion of validation of scientific explanations (see also Maturana and Varela 1988, Maturana 1990, and Appendix 1). Therefore, the proposed generative mechanism becomes an explanation in the act of being accepted as such by an observer—who in practice can be the same person that proposes it.

In these circumstances, if one wants to explain human beings and human life, what one has to do is to propose a generative mechanism that will give rise to human life and to all aspects of human beingness as a result of its operation. Moreover, if one wants such a generative mechanism to be accepted or rejected as an explanation in its own terms, one must make explicit the informal condition that defines the domain in which one claims it to be valid. Accordingly, because we want to speak about human beings as biological entities and we want to explain their origin as such, we have to propose a biological generative mechanism such that the human manner of living and human beingness may result as a consequence of its operation. Furthermore, because we want to propose a scientific explanation of human beingness, we have to do so in a way that satisfies the criterion of validation of scientific explanations (see Appendix 1). Moreover, in this essay our particular task is to propose a mechanism not only for the generation of the human lineage, but also for the occurrence of the features of our modern human cultural life. And we want to do so in a way that reveals the extent to which our peculiar present way of living in the recurrent conflicts of love and aggression, peace and war, is either a basic aspect of our biological life or a result of the cultural history that gave origin to us.

Lineaging

The history of living beings on earth is the history of the origin, establishment, diversification through ramification, and extinction of lineages, under conditions in which a lineage is defined and constituted by the reproductive conservation of an ontogenic phenotype, or manner of living, through a succession of generations. The ontogenic phenotype is the particular configuration of dynamic relations between organism and medium that an organism lives from its inception to its death. That is, the ontogenic phenotype is the manner in which an organism happens to live its life as a configuration of dynamic structural changes and relations that entail what happens in the organism, the medium, and in their relations, rather than a succession of particular events. Moreover, it is because when we speak of the conservation of an ontogenic phenotype in the constitution of a lineage we refer to the reproductive conservation of a configuration of processes and not to any particular case, that we call the ontogenic phenotype conserved in a lineage also the manner of living that defines the lineage.

Accordingly, what one identifies when one identifies a species or a particular kind of living system or organism, is a manner of living that is conserved generation after generation through the reproduction of the organisms that realize that manner of living under the particular circumstances in which they live. Therefore, when a new particular manner of living begins to be conserved generation after generation through the reproduction of the living beings that realize it, a new lineage arises as well as the circumstances in which it is conserved (see also Maturana and Mpodozis, 2000). In general terms, one can say that whenever a particular configurations of relations begins to be conserved among a collection of elements, either in the internal dynamics of a system, or in the interactions between systems, all else becomes open to change. This is a systemic condition that pertains in any part of the cosmos as long as there structural determinism. It is the basic dynamic condition or fundament that makes possible the conservation and change of manners of living in both individuals and in the evolutionary history of living systems.

Although many biologists may not agree with what we think, we claim that the reproduction and reproductive conservation of a manner of living in the constitution of a lineage, is a systemic process that involves dynamic relations between the organisms and the medium, and not a process determined by a molecular system of inheritance as is usually thought when speaking of genetic determination with DNA as the molecules of inheritance (see Appendix 3).

What the genetic constitution of an organism determines is at most its initial structure, and through that initial structure, the diversity of the possible particular ontogenic phenotypes that the organism can live in its interactions in the medium. The genetic constitution does not determine which particular ontogenic phenotype an organism will live, or indeed lives, at any moment. The particular ontogenic phenotype in fact lived by an organism as it interacts in a medium arises systemically moment by moment through the structural changes that the organism and the medium trigger in each other in their recurrent interactions. And this occurs as a process in which the organism and the medium spontaneously change together congruently following a path of structural changes in which the organism and the medium remain in a dynamic structural relation of operational congruence or co-adaptation. This process of congruent changes of the organism and medium continues as a spontaneous dynamics as long as the organism conserves its organization as a living system as well as its relation of operational congruence (adaptation) with the medium through its recurrent interactions. When either the living organization or the adaptation of the organism to the medium (co-adaptation) is lost, the ontogeny of the organism comes to its end as it dies.

A particular ontogenic phenotype is conserved as a lineage through reproduction only as long as realization of the manner of living which gives rise to that phenotype contributes to create the conditions under which it can be repeated in the next generation. A lineage arises only if the realization of a manner of living by an organism brings forth in its offspring, and contributes, directly or indirectly, to bring forth in the medium the condition under which that particular manner of living can be repeated. Thus the constitution of a lineage is a systemic process or phenomenon that involves both organism and medium, and not a phenomenon of genetic or molecular determination.

The process of systemic realization of a manner of living or ontogenic phenotype is called in biology epigenesis, and we call the relational dynamics of its realization, ontogenic structural drift. At the same time, we call the systemic reproductive conservation of a manner of living and or of its variations, phylogenic structural drift, and we claim that that which we biologists connote as we speak of evolution is or occurs in a process of phylogenic structural drift. For a more detailed view, see Appendix 3.

Due to the systemic character of the epigenesis of an organism, two different genetic constitutions that allow for the epigenetic realization of the same manner of living in two organisms of the same species or kind are indistinguishable from the perspective of such realization. And this is so, of course, even though the actual inner dynamic structures of the two organisms are different as a result of their different genetic constitutions and independent epigenesis. At the same time, any feature of the realization of the ontogeny of an organism that arises in its living as a habit that conserves a particular organism medium relation, and which is conserved in the offspring of that organism also as a similar learned habit that conserves the relational conditions for its similar conservation in the next generation, will form part of a manner of living henceforth conserved, and will be a feature of the ontogenic phenotype that defines a new lineage, or a variation of an old lineage, around which everything else becomes open to change.

Finally, and in general terms, we claim that the systemic reproductive conservation of a manner of living and the resulting constitution of a lineage unavoidably lead to the conservation of genetic variations in the lineage whose participation in the epigenesis of the organism does not interfere with the conservation of the manner of living that defines it. Moreover, in the course of the generations of the lineage, and through their epigenic interplay with the rest of the genetic constitution of the members of the lineage, those genetic variations may become co-opted into the realization and conservation of the manner of living that defines the lineage. Furthermore, the participation of those genetic variations will remain invisible through the systemic conservation of the manner of living that defines a lineage until their epigenic interplay with other genetic variations, or with the circumstances of the medium in which the epigenesis takes place, results in a change in the manner of living realized by some members of the lineage. If that happens, and this new manner of living indeed begins to be reproduced systemically, and thus conserved generation after generation, a new lineage arises that co-opts those genetic variations for its systemic conservation. The basic consequences of all this that are relevant for our purpose, can be summarized as follows:

1. Many different genetic constitutions can participate in the epigenetic realization of the same ontogenic phenotype because this is systemically realized in the epigenesis of each individual, as well as systemically conserved when defining a lineage, and is not genetically determined. As a result, two things will always be happening: (a) all genetic variations whose participation in the epigenesis do not interfere with the conservation of the manner of living that defines a lineage will be conserved in it as irrelevant inclusions, or will be lost, or will become co-opted in its realization; and (b) as a new lineage arises, the genetic constitution of the organisms that form it will change following a path of genetic drift bounded by the systemic conservation of the ontogenic phenotype that defines the lineage.

2. As a particular manner of living is conserved generation after generation in a lineage, all the features of the

realization of the living of the members of the lineage that are not aspects of the manner of living systemically conserved become open to change as irrelevant variations of the lineage.

3. When a particular variation in the ontogenic phenotype that defines a lineage begins to be systemically conserved generation after generation, a new lineage arises. This is something that happens regardless of whether the variation arises as a result of genetic or non-genetic changes in the structures of the reproducing organisms, or as a result of some changes in the dynamic regularities of the medium, or as a result of both, because the constitution of a lineage is a systemic phenomenon, not a genetic one.

4. The systemic conservation of the ontogenic phenotype that defines a lineage sets systemic boundary conditions for the conservation of the genetic variations in the members of that lineage through their differential survival in the realization of that ontogenic phenotype. The result of this differential survival is either extinction of some lineages, or the establishment of new ones as indicated in point 3. As a consequence, the conservation of the manner of living that defines a lineage guides the course of the genetic drift that takes place in the history of a lineage. We call the systemic process through which old lineages are conserved and new lineages arise *phylogenic drift* or *phylogenetic structural drift*. For more insight in our thinking about systemic reproduction and the matter of genetic determination, see Appendix 3.

In these circumstances, if we want to explain our human origin, we must propose as a generative mechanism the systemic conservation of a manner of living. In other words we must propose the basic manner of living that we think gave origin through successive conserved variation to the system of lineages of bipedal primates of which we are now a living branch.

Domains of Existence

Let us now apply what we have said so far (even if to some extent we repeat) to the explanation of our origin as human beings. We human beings as living systems are molecular systems, and as molecular systems we are structure determined systems. In a structure determined system an observer distinguishes its organization as the configuration of relations that define its class identity, and its structure as the relations and components that realize it as a particular case of its class (see Appendix 2). A constitutive feature of structure determined systems is that external agents do not specify what happens in them. External agents may trigger structural changes in such systems, but the nature of the changes are determined by the structure of the system at the moment when they encounter the external agents. Since we humans are structure determined systems we adhere to this constitutive feature: namely the external agents that impinge upon us can only trigger in us structural changes determined in us.

Structural determinism is not an ontological assumption, nor is it an *a priori* explanatory notion; it is an abstraction from the regularities of our experiences as we operate as the kind of living systems that we are as human beings, and that we make as observers as we use our experiences to explain our experiences. As such, structural determinism is the operational fundament for all that we do in any experiential domain as we use the coherences of our experiences to explain our experiences in it. Moreover, structural determinism as the fundament of our operation as living systems, is in general terms a constitutive condition of the realization of the living system of living systems. In these circumstances, as we do whatever we do in the realization of our living as structure determined systems, structural determinism is both the condition of possibility and the fundament for our explaining and understanding of living systems in general, as well as for the explaining and the understanding of ourselves as human beings, in particular (see Appendix 2).

As a result of its condition as structure determined system, a living system exists in the structural dynamics of its bodyhood as this is realized in a flow of continuous structural changes. As such, a living system is constituted as a unity or totality that exists in a closed dynamics of structural changes in the conservation of living, which we refer to as *operational closure*. The realization of the living system in its closed dynamics of structure, as molecular system open to the flow of matter and energy through them, generates a progression of states of living as long as these systems are alive. Due to this condition, the life history of a living system is a history of structural changes contingent to internal structural dynamics of the living system as well as to the structural changes triggered in it by its interactions in the medium, and it is a history that lasts as long as the living of the living system is conserved through those structural changes. In other words, the life history, or ontogenic structural drift of a living system, lasts only as long as it follows a course in which the living system remains alive through the structural changes that it undergoes both as a result of its internal structural dynamics and as a result of its interactions in the medium. If this does not happen, the living system dies and its life history comes to an end. So living occurs in the flow of the structural changes of the living system as long as its structure and the structure of the medium change together congruently in the conservation of living (conservation of adaptation), and lasts as long as that dynamic structural congruence between the living system and the medium is conserved in the conservation of living (conservation of organization).

At the same time, due to their structural determinism and to their internally closed dynamics of states, living systems operate as totalities in the domain of interactions (medium) where they exist as singular entities in the realization of their living. The interaction space or medium in which a living system exists arises together with the living system in its distinction by the observer as the domain of existence that contains it. It is in the medium, and as part of the medium, that an observer distinguishes a living system as a behaving singular entity as he or she interacts with it. In these circumstances, the medium is, in the distinction of the observer, all that does not form part of the structure of a living system, and it has as such an operational existence as all that does not form part of the structural realization of the living systems that it contains, and it exists as the domain of all the actual and potential interactions in which the living system can be imagined to participate. As such, the medium is also a dynamic structure determined system that has a changing structure, which follows a course of change contingent both to its own independent structural dynamics, and to the structural changes triggered in it by its interactions with the living systems that it contains.

A living system, therefore, exists as a system in two non-intersecting operational domains. One is the domain of its structure, that is, the domain of operation of the elements that are its components as they compose it, constituting it as a totality. The other is the domain where it interacts as a whole, or totality, through the operation of its properties as a totality as these arise in its interactions as a totality in the medium. The domain where a living system exists and operates as a totality, though, arises with its constitution as a living system, as the observer distinguishes the living system as a whole by interacting with it as it operates as a totality in the domain where it exists as such. In these circumstances, as the observer distinguishes (sees, hears, touches, smells) a living systems as a living system (a totality), he or she distinguishes it endowed with certain properties that arise with the living system as he or she distinguishes it as such. But, as the observer explains the properties of the living system as they arise in his or her distinction of it, it becomes apparent to him or her that those properties are realized through the operation of the properties of the elements that compose it as a structure determined entity. Thus, for example, as we human beings interact in a conversation we interact as totalities with words, signs and symbols in the relational domain of language, yet as we look at the process of our interactions in language, we see that as

composite entities we interact through the operation of the properties of the cells and molecules that compose us.
In summary:
1. The operational domain in which a living system exists as a whole is different from the operational domain in which it exists as a composite entity, and these two operational domains do not intersect.
2. The operational domain in which a living system exists a whole results from the operation of the elements that realize it as a composite entity, but is not determined by them. This operational domain arises as the living system operates as a totality. Such a domain is the medium, and a living system exists as long as its organization and adaptation are conserved through the flow of its interactions in the medium.
3. As a living system interacts as a totality, it undergoes structural changes triggered in it through the operation of the elements that compose it. So, although the two domains in which a living systems exists, the domain of its composition and the domain in which it operates as a totality, do not intersect, they modulate each other through the structural change that living system and medium undergo through their recursive interactions (see also Appendix 2).

It is in the domain where a living system exists as a totality that the observer distinguishes it in behavior as he or she sees it in dynamic relations with the medium. Behavior, however, is not something that the living system does; behavior is what happens in the interactions of the living system with the medium. Indeed, behavior happens as a dynamic configuration of interrelations between living system and medium that takes place through the changes of structure of the living system and the changes of structure of the medium in the flow of their recurrent interactions. Behavior involves both living system and the medium. Or, said more precisely, behavior is a dynamic interactional and relational flow that an observer distinguishes as taking place between living system and medium, and that occurs through the realization of the living of the living system.

That is, behavior takes place in the encounter of the living system and the medium, and is a dynamic flow of relational changes that arises involving both the living system and the medium, and not as something that the living system does by itself (Figure 2.1).

As each structural change in the organism follows a course modulated only moment after moment by the

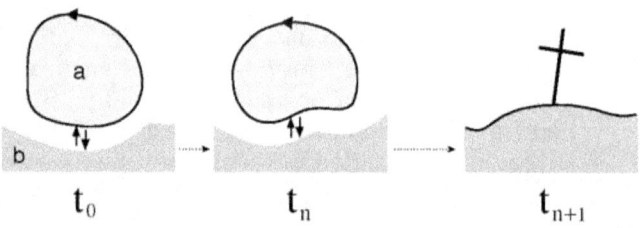

Fig. 2.1. In ontogenic structural drift the organism (a) and the medium (b) exist in recursive interactions beginning at time to and continuing through time t_n. This results in a history of congruent structural changes in both, as indicated by the fit between the changing shapes in this figure. This history of changes courses in the conservation of both organization and adaptation in the living system until it dies at t_{n+1}.

sequence of its interactions in the medium, so also each structural change in the medium follow a course contingent to the flow of its interactions with the organisms that it contains, without specifying them. The result is that the recurrent interactions between living system and medium constitute a recursive dynamics in which each encounter between the living system and the medium triggers in each of them a structural change that occurs on top of the previous structural change in a manner in which they cannot be anything but congruent with each other.

The dynamic structure of the organisms and the dynamic structure of the medium in which these exist in recurrent interactions, change together congruently as a spontaneous consequence of those recursive interactions, and it is the structural congruence between living system and medium that arises in this way that we call structural coupling. Moreover, such congruence arises spontaneously in the recurrent interactions between a living system and the medium that contains it as a simple result of the interplay of their otherwise independent structural dynamics, and lasts as long as the living system conserves its organization and does not disintegrate. All this we have said or implied above. But what we want to add here, is that as a result of the dynamics of structural coupling, whenever there is a collection of living systems that form a network of direct and indirect recursive interactions in the realization of their living, a biosphere arises as a closed network of multidimensional reciprocal structural couplings that includes all the living systems as well as all the non-living features of the medium that participate in it. Furthermore, we also wish to add that when a biosphere is formed, the living systems that compose it change together in a way such that whenever an observer looks at them, he or she finds them generating a behavior always adequate to the dynamic circumstances in which they are as a simple result of their history of structural coupling. The dimensions involved in structural coupling can be any, but they can only be seen or revealed through the operation of the living systems in their domains of interactions. Accordingly, the observer discovers them through the operation of the living system, and describes them in terms of the consequences in his or her experiential domain of interfering with them in his or her interactions with it (see Appendix 2 for more details).

The interplay of the structural changes of the organism and the medium that we have just described above occurs interrelating the two phenomenal domains in which a living system exists through dynamic generative relations, and not through the local determinations that one expects when one deals with the interactions between elements of the same domain. As a living system interacts as a whole through the operation of the properties of its components, its structure follows a course of structural changes congruent with the structural changes of the medium. Further-

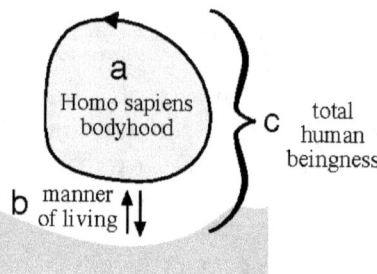

Fig. 2.2 We human beings exist as biological entities in our bodyhood (a) and in the realization of our humanness in our relational space (b). Our total human beingness (c) takes place in the recursive interplay between these two domains.

more, it is the course of interactions that conserves the living of the living system, and determines the course followed by the congruent structural changes of the living system and the medium. Therefore, although the two operational domains in which a living system exists do not intersect, and neither can be deduced from or reduced to the other, each operational domain depends dynamically on the other, as they are structurally related through the dynamics of structural coupling of the organism and the medium.

What happens with us human beings in these circumstances? How and where do we exist? Do we also exist in two domains or more, and how? As biological entities, or better, as the kinds of zoological entities that we are, we are in our bodyhoods *Homo sapiens sapiens*, and we exist in our structural dynamics as such (Figure 2.2a). As the kind of animals that we are, namely, according to the manner we live our humanness, we exist and operate as human beings in a relational space (Figure 2.2b). We are human beings as a totality (Figure 2.2c) as we live our bodyhoods of *Homo sapiens sapiens* in the realization of our humanness through our behavior as human beings. Thus we human beings exist in the recursive interplay of our bodyhoods and our human realization. Said more formally, we human beings exist in continuous structural changes in the systemic recursive conservation of our individual human relational characteristics.

Furthermore, we each exist as part of the medium for each other. Thus in any relation between two human beings follows the same dynamics of recursive systemic changes in which both beings change congruently together, as long as they impinge on each other recursively (Figure 2.3). In this way our *Homo sapiens sapiens* dynamic structure changes along a course that is modulated by our living together as humans. Human bodyhoods (Figure 2.3 a and b) and human manners of living (Figure 2.3 c) change congruently with each other as a mere consequence of being structure determined systems in recursive interaction with each other, while simultaneously changing congruently with the rest of our medium.

So, as human beings we are neither our bodyhoods, nor our behavior, rather we are a continuous systemic dynamics that takes place in the interplay between bodyhood and behavior, and we exist as languaging beings in a relational space that arises in that dynamics. Indeed, all systems exist like this, each according to its own manner of relating as a totality in a relational space that arises through its continuous recursive interactions in the medium while it conserves its organization and adaptation through the flow of its

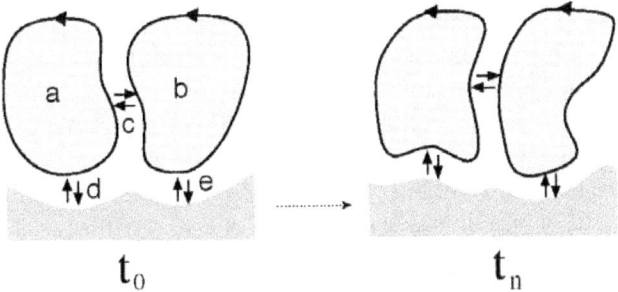

Fig. 2.3 Two human beings exist as biological entities in their bodyhood (a and b) and in the realization of their humanness in the relational space between them (c) while also realizing their humanness through the recursive co-modulation with the rest of their medium (d and e).

structural changes. Under these circumstances, human beings, as is the case with all living systems, with systems in general, with the biosphere, and with the cosmos itself, exist in their continuous realization as structure determined systems in a permanent, changing present. Furthermore, human beings (as is the case with all composite entities) exist through their many dimensions of interactions as participants of the interrelated congruent structural changes that interconnect all the elements that constitute the changing present that the cosmos is as a web of dynamic structural couplings.

It is this condition of constitution of living beings in general, and of human beings in particular as a permanent changing present, that makes human existence a historical process. At the same time, this condition makes the present of each human being at any moment an aspect of the present in the history of structural changes of the biosphere that arises with his or her participation. In these circumstances, we human beings live now a present that is happening in an expansion of the human presence that is transforming the earth's biosphere into an homosphere or human-centered ecosystem.

Languaging

Language is a manner of living in recurrent interactions in a flow of coordinations of coordinations of consensual behaviors. Consensual does not refer to consent, but is that coordination of behavior which takes place in a flow of coherent transformations in the absence of stipulation, as in the case of agreement. Coordination of behavior happens without language throughout the biosphere. It is the recursion on coordination, that is coordination of coordinations, which constitutes language. When we speak of "languaging" as a verb, we are referring to the recursive flow of consensual coordinations of behaviors.

Furthermore, we human beings exist in the braiding of languaging and emotioning. That is, our emotioning changes in the course of our languaging, and our languaging changes in the course of our emotioning (see Maturana, 1988). We call this braiding of languaging and emotioning *conversation*.

If we attend at what we do in daily life as we do whatever we do with other human beings, we may notice that we move in our recursive interactions with them in coordinations of coordinations of behaviors. And we can see that we acknowledge as languaging that which happens in the flow of our recursive coordinations of behavior. Furthermore, if we look more deeply in the circumstances in which a child becomes a languaging being, we may also notice that the coordinations of coordinations of behaviors in which we participate as we flow in languaging, arise in our living together in a manner generated in the particularities of our living together, and that as such they are consensual. Languaging occurs in consensuality. Consensuality happens as a spontaneous coordination of behavior that does not require language to occur. Thus it is totally different from agreement, which is a stipulated coordination of behavior that arises only through languaging. As we reflect on what an agreement is, we may also notice that operations such as declarations, statements, expressions, promises, or requests, as well as orientations such as purposes, intentions, or desires, are also all secondary operations in languaging. We can distinguish them as such as we reflect on what we do once we are already living in language, and thus they are not primary constitutive elements of language.

If we continue in this reflection, we may further notice that the particular configurations of sounds, gestures, or marks that we call words are operational nodes in the network of consensual coordinations of coordinations of behaviors that we live as languaging beings. And we may also notice that the meaning of a word as a particular configuration of sounds, gestures, or marks takes place in the flow of coordinations of behaviors in which it participates as an element in the flow of consensual coordinations of coordinations of behaviors that languaging is. That this is indeed the case is shown in any dictionary, where one can see that each of the different meanings given to any particular word corresponds to a different manner in which that word orients or guides the flow of the coordinations of behaviors and emotions taking place in a conversation.

The consensual coordinations of consensual coordinations of behavior, which constitutes languaging, is a recursive dynamics in the domain of coordination of consensual behaviors. When a cyclical process becomes coupled to a linear one, the phenomenon of recursion takes place, and whenever a recursive dynamics begins, a completely new phenomenal domain arises. Walking is an example. Walking arises when a cyclical movement of some body appendages become coupled with the linear displacement of the medium. Once this coupling took place and walking appeared in the history of living systems, a completely new manner of living appeared that became expanded in an open-ended evolutionary process of diversification in the movements of displacement.

The same happened in the history that gave origin to us when the cyclical consensual coordinations of behavior became coupled with the linear flow of the consequences of doing things together in consensual coordinations of behaviors. When that recursive dynamic happened as a manner of living in our ancestors, the new manner of living that arose as the flow of their living consensual coordinations of behavior, was languaging. As a domain of living in recursive consensual coordinations of behavior, languaging constitutes an expanding field of open-ended possibilities for the recursive generation of new manners of living together. Furthermore, as languaging arose, it arose interlaced with a living in consensual coordinations of emotions in what we have called conversations. Accordingly, when languaging became a manner of living conserved generation after generation in the learning of the children, it became so as a manner of living together in a network of conversations.

What must have occurred is that occasional episodes of languaging as circumstantial occasions of coordinations of coordinations of behavior in the daily life of our ancestors began to be conserved spontaneously, generation after generation, as a natural feature of their manner of living in the learning of the children. At the start, the new manner of living in language would not have constituted for the participants something remarkable, as it must have been only a change in the manner of doing together what they were doing together anyhow. Furthermore, the many new domains of consensual coordinations of behaviors that could arise as a simple result of the conservation of living together in small groups of enjoyable intimacy in consensual coordinations of consensual coordinations of behavior, were initially only a historical possibility. From the perspective of the worlds that we now bring about in our living in language, we may see languaging as a great advantage for doing things together, but the living in language of our ancestors did not arise because it was necessary or advantageous in any way. We claim that what must have happened is that as episodes of languaging began to be systemically conserved generation after generation in the learning of the children, a new lineage arose, and everything began to change in the history of that new lineage around the conservation of languaging as the manner of living that defined it. Nothing happens, and nothing has happened, in the history of living systems because it was necessary, but as some new manner of living begins to be systemically conserved, everything else (including the genetic system) becomes open to change round what is conserved. We modern human beings are the present of a phylogenic drift, not an attainment.

Let us now consider an example of a minimal case of languaging in our daily living. When we take a dog to live with us and we give it a name, we can claim that the dog knows its name when it orients to us as we call it by name, but only as we say "come" or make some particular gesture, it comes to us. If it were to come directly on hearing its name, this could well be simply a suitable coordination of behavior, not the coordination of the coordination of behavior entailed in knowing one's name. When a dog learns its name, what has happened is that a coordination of coordination of behavior has become established through our living with the dog in recurrent interactions, simply in the pleasure of living together. In the life of the dog this example of language is a mere episode, while in us human beings language is a feature of our human living. We human beings live languaging, and languaging is our manner of living.

What is significant for the constitution of a new lineage through a shift in some aspect of the manner of living of the members of an already existing one, is not any particular episode of that new feature in the living of some members of that lineage. It is the reappearance, generation after generation, of the new feature as a characteristic of the manner of living conserved through its systemic reproduction that constitutes the new lineage. In our case, what must have made us humans was not the episodic occurrence of languaging situations similar to that described above with our dog, but the systemic conservation of living together in recurrent and recursive conversations through the learning of the children of our ancestors. If that happened, and we claim that it must have happened, a space was opened for everything else to change around the conservation of living in conversations as the manner of living that henceforth defined the system of lineages of which we are a present case. Therefore, saying that we are languaging beings, or saying that what defines us or makes us human beings is our living in language, means that to live languaging is the manner of living that is systemically conserved, generation after generation, through the learning of our children in our lineage.

From all that we have said it should be apparent that languaging is not an abstract activity, it is a domain of doings. We could also say that languaging is a flow of living together in consensual coordinations of consensual coordinations of doings. Because of this our life has the shape of our languaging, and the theoretical reflections that we live are operationally effective in the operational domain in which they apply as we operate in our doings through them in the domains of doings which they connote. In these circumstances, in order to explain the origin of humanness, we have to propose the historical relational scenario in which we think languaging could have arisen and could have begun to be systemically conserved generation after generation in our ancestors.

Objects

Our daily experience is that we distinguish entities as if they existed independently from our distinguishing them. However, as structure determined systems, all that we distinguish arises in our structural dynamics determined by our structural dynamics, and not according to any external entity that an observer may see impinging on us. Our feeling of existing in a domain of independent external entities is not denied, but the explanation of this feeling is not that we indeed have the ability to distinguish external entities. A similar case occurs with our daily experience of seeing that the sun rises in the east at dawn and moves over us in the sky to settle in the west. This feeling is not explained through the claim that indeed the sun does this; rather we accept the explanation that the earth is rotating from the west to the east while we look at the sun. The explanation based on the earth's rotation does not deny our feeling that we remain still while the sun moves. Similarly, the feeling that objects are external to us even though we cannot claim that we distinguish them as such is not denied by the explanation that objects arise in languaging, rather than having an independent existence.

Objects arise in language as coordinations of coordinations of doings that constitute a field of shared coordinations of doings that we call a *domain of interobjectivity* , and which is felt by those who live it as a *domain of shared entities*. To those who live in a domain of interobjectivity the shared entities feel like fully external entities because through their recursive coordinations of doings, the entitites appear through being lived in the same way by all those who live those recursive coordination of doings. In other words, the experience of "objects" is how we feel our coordinations of coordinations of doings as we operate in a domain of interobjectivity. It is to this feeling that we as observers refer when we speak of objects.

Moreover, it is because of this that we usually refer to language (in a reflection in language about language) as a domain of descriptions of objects, or of communications about objects, as if these were independent entities. As human beings we exist in language. To say that we exist in language means that we do not exist in our bodyhood, nor in our behavior, but in a flow of recursive coordinations of consensual behaviors that modulate the course of the flow of our body dynamics while our body dynamics modulates the course of the flow of our behavior in the continuous generation of changing domains of interobjectivity. It is through existing as languaging beings that observing and the observer arise as a manner of being in the flow of interobjectivity in which our recursive coordinations of doings result in the coordinations of coordinations of our coordinations of doings. This means that the domain of existence in languaging is a domain of shared objects in interobjectivity.

It is under the premise that objects are entities with an independent existence, that the notion of self-distinction appears as a problem in the modern philosophy of language. Under this premise the very notion of a self requires that the self be an entity independent of and external to the observer who distinguishes it, and who is able to distinguish it precisely because it is independent and external. But the self in self-distinction is not an entity independent of the observer who makes the distinction, and cannot be so because what is indicated in self-distinction is that it is the self that is distinguished who makes the distinction. This difficulty resolves as soon as it becomes apparent to the observer that the domain of existence in languaging is a domain of shared entities that appears as a domain of independent objects, but which in fact occurs as a space of interobjectivity as a domain of shared consensual coordinations of doings in a flow of coexistence in coordinations of coordinations of consensual behaviors.

As one of us (Verden-Zöller, in Maturana and Verden-Zöller, 1993) has shown, the world that a child lives, and that we later live as adults, is a world in which he or she arises in self-operational knowledge in his or her relations of play with the mother and father. The initial operational knowledge of his or her body, which arises through movement and mutual touching in playing and caressing, becomes expanded as self-description, self-distinction, and self-consciousness when the child begins to live in language. As the mother plays with the child, languaging begins to appear in the course of their interactions in the flow of the coordinations of coordinations of doings that the mother generates and guides. As this happens, things, the parts of the child's body, and the child all arise as objects through recursive consensual coordinations of behavior. In other words, the self arises in the same way as any other object in the domain of interobjectivity.

For example, a fruit arises as a shared coordination of doings as a shared entity, as an object, in the flow of the recursive consensual coordinations of behavior in the mother/child relationship in the play of handling, passing, and naming. It is in the actual flow of recursive consensual coordinations of doings that the fruit arises as an object through an operation in the particular domain of interobjectivity that the child lives with his or her mother. The nose of the child arises similarly as a shared coordination of doings, that is as an object, through the play of touching and naming. But the distinction by the child of his or her own nose, although it happens in the same manner as the distinction of any object, is an act of self-distinction in which the self (in this case an element of it) arises in the domain of shared entities as if it were an object independent of, as well as external to the observer who makes the distinction. Therefore, the self arises as such in the same way in which any other object arises in the domain of interobjectivity. Yet, since the self does not arise as an external manipulable entity in the same operational domain that a fruit arises as such, what also arises with the self-distinction is an entirely new relational domain in the creation of a new domain of interobjectivity, namely the domain of reflexive distinctions, and through it, the domain of self-consciousness.

Emotioning

We move in daily life from one emotion or mood to another; we change emotions and moods as our living goes by. If we attend to what we connote or distinguish in daily life when we distinguish moods or emotions, we may notice that we always refer to what the person, or the non-human animal that we are considering, may do, and we speak in terms of the kinds of doings that it may generate without indicating any particular one. In other words, we claim here that what we distinguish as observers when we distinguish an emotion or a mood is a domain of relational behaviors, and not a particular doing. We also claim that when we distinguish an emotion or a mood in any human or non-human animal, we connote by implication the full anatomical and physiological dynamics that determines the domain of relational behaviors in which the human or non-human animal moves at that moment.

In a way, a change of emotion or mood is a change of brain and body. Through different emotions human and non-human animals become different beings, beings that see differently, hear differently, move and act differently. In particular, we human beings become different rational beings, and we think, reason, and reflect differently as our emotions change. We move in the drift of our living following a path guided by our emotions. As we interact our emotions may change; as we talk our emotions may change; as we reflect our emotions may change; as we act our emotions may change; as we think our emotions may change; as we emotion ... our emotions may change. Moreover, as our emotions constitute the grounding of all our doings, they guide our living. Indeed, as our emotions change, we become different beings in our emotioning and in our reasoning, and we live the flow of our emotioning most of the time without being aware of our changes.

We claim that it is the emotion or mood, that is, the domain of relational behavior in which a particular doing takes place, that gives that doing its character as a particular action. Furthermore, we also claim here that the different emotions or moods that we live can be fully characterized in terms of the kinds of relational behaviors that they entail as domains of actions. For example, the emotion of love as a domain of actions, is the domain of those relational behaviors through which another arises as a legitimate other in coexistence with oneself. Similarly, the emotion of aggression as a domain of actions, is the domain of those relational behaviors through which another is denied as a legitimate other in coexistence with oneself. Emotions are realized in themselves, that is, in the actual operation of the living system in the relational domain that constitutes them. Thus, love is realized in loving, aggression is realized in aggression.

To act in a way that the other arises as a legitimate other does not mean blind acceptance, it only means that the other does not need to justify its existence. When this is the case a relation is possible without prejudice, and both liking and not liking take place in full open responsibility. Liking or not liking another, according to what one sees without the distortion of a prejudice, and acting in responsibility for one's liking or not liking, are acts in love. Contrary to this, negating another according to what one imagines or supposes or wants the other to be, are acts in aggression.

Emotions create the systemic relational dynamics which conserve them, and a change of emotion entails a basic shift in the systemic relational dynamics of the participants. Different emotions entail different relational behaviors. Let us see two examples: power relations and love relations. It is apparent from what we have said, that the emotion of love is realized in the relational behavior of the lover only, as the loved one arises as a legitimate other through the behavior of the lover without necessarily being an active participant in a loving or any other relation with the lover. Because of this love is intrinsically unidirectional, and liberates—that is love lets the other be even in the act of separation. Power, on the other hand, is bi-directional as it takes place in a relation of domination and submission that entails self negation of both participants. The one that dominates negates him or herself as an autonomous being by acting as if his or her superiority were intrinsic to him or her, and the one that submits negates him or herself in the act of submission. Relations of power create resentment. Love, as it operates in self-respect and self-acceptance, brings with itself well being.

Emotions as domains of relational behaviors constitute the relational space in which they exist and are conserved. Thus, relations of power exist in the negation of the other (who could be oneself), and those who like to be in them must live in the continuous creation and recreation of relations of domination over others. The result is that relations of power continuously slide into tyranny, and tyranny conserves relations of domination and submission. Relations of love generate freedom and invite collaboration, even when due to their uni-directionality they are lonely. As a result love generates the conditions for love through the well being that it generates, and when love is reciprocated companionship may result. Love is visionary, not blind, and through the vision that it entails it brings forth the relational space of love.

The emotion we find ourselves in at any instant creates the relational conditions which conserve that emotion through penetrating all our doings at that instant. However, the emotion we are in may change when some inter-current circumstance, which may be a reflection, triggers a shift in the flow of our relational dynamics (see Appendix 10, for further reflections on love).

In daily life the words emotion and mood connote our distinction of different durations in our operation in the different relational domains in which we may live. Thus, the word "mood" connotes a much longer duration than the word "emotion". Emotions and moods constitute at every instant the relational background in which the life of an animal takes place as it lives. Moreover, it is the dynamic configuration of changing emotions and moods, which characterizes the manner of living systemically conserved in a lineage, that determines the manner of relating of the members of the lineage along their lives.

The actual emotioning that the members of a lineage live as individuals along their lives is what specifies the evolutionary course that a lineage may follow as the emotioning determines the course of the living of an organism, and how and where its descendents may come to live. Therefore, in order to understand and explain the origin of humanness, it is necessary to generate a view of the background of emotioning in our pre-human ancestors. To be adequate this view should include the variations in the way these ancestors lived their individual lives, as any occasional manners of relating which were systemically conserved along the generations, also made possible and gave origin to the manner of living that defines the lineage to which we modern human beings belong.

Conversations

We claim that humanness began when in a particular family, or in a small group of families of our ancestors, language began to be conserved systemically as a manner of living generation after generation in the learning of the children. And we claim that as that happened, and languaging became the central feature of the manner of living conserved generation after generation around which everything else could change in the history of that or those families, our lineage arose. Furthermore, we think that languaging must have begun to be conserved as a manner of living immersed in the configuration of emotioning of the living together that made possible and constituted the nearness and permanence of coexistence in which it was possible that living in consensual coordinations of consensual coordinations of behaviors could take place as well as be conserved from generation to generation.

Moreover, we think that living in languaging must have arisen spontaneously braided with the emotioning of the family in which it began as a simple consequence of the closed intimacy of the living together of the small ancestral families of our lineage. The manner of emotioning that animals like us (primates in particular, and mammals in general) live along their lives is fundamentally consensual, so the braiding of languaging and emotioning that began with our lineage must have arises consensually, and been respectively conserved or open to change according to the emotioning of the families that began to live in language.

As we have already said, we call this consensual braiding of languaging and emotioning *conversation*, and we think that what began, when humanness began in the transgenerational conservation of the braiding of languaging and emotioning, was a living in conversations as the manner of living that defined our lineage. As a consequence, all that we human beings do as human beings, takes place in networks of conversation. Human existence takes place in the flow of conversations in the braiding of recursive consensual coordinations of doings and domains of relational behaviors, and that what takes place through us outside conversations, is not human action.

The biblical myth of the Tower of Babel is perhaps a good case of common knowledge that fully reveals what we mean. This myth says that human beings wanted to make a tower that would reach Heaven, and that God, seeing what they were doing, and not liking it, interfered with the construction by confusing their tongues. After this divine act, the tower could not be completed.

We think that the building of the Tower of Babel as a human activity was a network of conversations, and that what God did was to confuse the conversations. That is, he not only confused the languages but also the emotions, so that they could not agree around the desire to build the tower, or on how this should be done. If the desire for building the tower had been conserved, the humans would have invented a conversation that would have made building the tower possible.

The basic historical result of our living in conversations has been a recursive expansion of our abilities to generate and to participate in any kind of conversation. Indeed, we claim that the evolutionary history of our human lineage has been a history of conservation and change in the networks of conversations in a way that has resulted in the constitution of many different cultures. Different cultures have been and are now lived as different closed networks of conversations that are different configurations of recursive consensual coordinations of doings and emotions.

Accordingly, if we want to explain our origin as human beings, as well as our present cultural existence we have two tasks. First we have to propose what we think was the nature of the history of evolutionary transformation in our ancestors that resulted in the arising of human beings as languaging animals, and second we have to propose a history that would give rise to the network of conversations that constitutes the particular manner of contradictory emotional existence that we humans live in the present. Our explanatory proposition should account for all the actual operational and emotional features of our cultural existence, as well as our ability to generate and participate in an open-ended variety of conversations.

Natural Drift

Living systems exist as individual living entities in the conservation of their organization as autopoietic systems (Varela, Maturana and Uribe, 1974, Maturana and Varela 1980), and form lineages that arise in the systemic reproductive conservation of different manners of living through which they are realized as different kinds of organisms. Accordingly, the history of terrestrial living systems is an uninterrupted history of the constitution, branching, conservation, and extinction of lineages of different manners of living. In this history, a new lineage arises when some particular variation in the manner of living of the members of an already existing lineage begins to be conserved from one generation to the next through systemic reproduction. This happens along with the conservation of the conditions of the medium that make possible the realization of the niche corresponding to the new manner of living that is being conserved. A lineage ends when the conditions for the systemic reproductive conservation of the realization of the manner of living that defines the lineage come to end. A lineage is established only when both the new organisms and their respective niches arise in the relational dynamics that simultaneously conserve the manner of living that defines the lineage and the conditions of the medium that make such a conservation possible. Hence, the history of living systems is necessarily a history in which organism and medium change together congruently.

The organism/medium relation whose conservation from one generation to the next defines and constitutes a lineage, is the *ontogenic phenotype/ontogenic niche relation* (Maturana and Mpodozis, 2000). In these circumstances, a lineage lasts only as long as the ontogenic phenotype/ontogenic niche relation that defines it is conserved through systemic reproduction. That is, the history of living systems is the history of the reproductive conservation of the co-adaptation of the living systems and the medium through the reproductive conservation of the organism/medium relations which conserve living as well as conserving variations in the manner of realization of the living under the form of different lineages.

The dynamic relations between organism and medium, in which a particular manner of living (or ontogenetic phenotype/ontogenetic niche relation) is conserved through reproduction, is named *systemic reproduction*. This is always a systemic process. Thus the actual realization of the manner of living that defines a lineage participates in constituting the systemic conditions for its continued realization and reproductive conservation in the lineage. This happens through the interplay of the structural changes of the living systems and the structural changes of the medium in which these living systems realize their niches. Given this, a lineage lasts until changes arise in the medium or in the members of the lineage that make the systemic reproductive conservation of the manner of living that defined the lineage impossible. When this happens, either the lineage stops, that is becomes extinct, or a shift is produced in the manner of living conserved henceforth. Hence a lineage is the spontaneous result of the systemic reproductive conservation of an ontogenic phenotype/ontogenic niche relation in a reproductive history of living systems in which living systems and medium change together congruently. This process of systemic reproductive conservation and change of the manners of living with the constitution and extinction of different lineages, is *phylogenic drift* (Maturana and Mpodozis, 2000).

One consequences of the constitution of a lineage through the systemic reproductive conservation of a manner of living (the ontogenic phenotype), is the production of evolutionary trends in which both the organisms and their medium change together in congruence around the conservation of some particular configuration of organism/medium. It is this relation that defines an otherwise changing lineage or system of lineages. Thus, for example, paleontology shows that the evolutionary history of horses took place in animals that walked on the tip of their toes as a trend of progressive loss of toes around the conservation and elongation of one toe in each leg, all associated with the conservation of the habit of running fast.

Another consequence of the systemic reproductive conservation of a manner of living is the extensive multiplication, diversification, and extinction of lineages that occurs through the ease with which a shift in the manner of living can be conserved or lost from one generation to the next. The overall result of this process of phylogenic drift is the differential survival of lineages in the process of evolution.

Darwin proposed the notion of *natural selection* as the mechanism that would explain this differential survival. He viewed competition as the driving force that led successive generations of organisms to become better adapted to their medium as the better adapted organisms left more offspring to carry on the lineage. In this view, the differential survival of different kinds of organisms and lineages are seen to emerge as the result of the operation of selective forces acting through selective advantages. The arising of the myriad different forms of adaptation, that is of the various different forms of operational congruence that exist between organisms and medium is seen to arise through the existence of various different selective forces leading to different selective advantages. The evolutionary history of living systems in this view is one of competitive struggle.

However, as we have described, in every moment phylogenic drift follows a path defined by the continuous conservation of organization and adaptation as an individual condition, not as a result of a comparative or competitive relation. Further, the differential survival of different lineages occurs as a spontaneous consequence of the conservation, or the lack of conservation, of living along the process of the actual living of the organisms, through the conservation or loss of their structural coupling with the medium — ot as a consequence of the application anything like a selective force. Accordingly that which is usually called *natural selection* in evolutionary biology is indeed the consequence of differential survival, but it is not the generative mechanism for the historical coherent transformation of organisms and medium in the course of the history of living systems. In other words, we (Maturana and Mpodozis, 2000) claim that the generative mechanism of biological evolution is what we have called *ontogenic and phylogenic natural drift*. The biological evolutionary process and the constitution of a biosphere begin spontaneously as soon as living systems arise and systemic reproduction occurs.

One of the consequences of using the notion of selective advantages to explain the different forms of living systems and their operational congruence with their conditions of existence is that one has to look for selective forces and comparative advantages in a domain of competition to show how they may have come about. Another consequence is that one remains bound to the implicit or explicit view which treats adaptation as a variable in the sense that an organism can be more or less adapted to the circumstances in which it lives. This view presumes that the circumstances of existence of an organism both preexist and are independent of the organism that lives these circumstances. Based on this way of thinking we look for the selective advantages that made possible the arising of language as a fundamental adaptation in the evolutionary history that gave origin to humanness. In this view language is generally proposed as a new adaptation that was necessary to give an otherwise poorly adapted species the possibility of survival.

We shall not look for selective advantages to explain our human origin. Our explanation will take into account that:

1. humans are structure determined systems; and
2. humans, like all living beings, exist in a continuously changing present in circumstances that arise with our living in the form of the niche that we inhabit; and
3. adaptation is not a variable but a constitutive constant relation of dynamic structural congruence between the living system and the medium that must be conserved for the living system to live; and
4. evolution takes place as a structural drift in the conservation of organization and adaptation.

Thus, to explain human origins we shall look at the structural and behavioral transformation around the conservation of some basic manner of living which would have made possible our origin in the primate lineage to which we belong. In doing this we shall look first for the manner of living which, through being conserved, constituted the trend that opened the path for our origin. Then we shall look for the conditions that gave rise to the conservation of those variations in that trend which eventually resulted in us as the kind of languaging animals that we humans presently are.

Chapter 3

Human Origins

Let us now come directly to our central concern: us human beings. Our basic question, as we indicated at the beginning, is: "How is it that we can live in mutual care, have ethical concerns, and at the same time deny all that through the rational justification of aggression?" We shall answer this basic question indirectly by providing a look into the fundaments of our biological constitution. We shall do this through answering two other questions to guide our reflections as we inquire into our evolutionary origin. These two questions are: "How did humanness begin?" and "How did we become the kind of animals that we are as human beings?" Yet, let us remember that we shall be looking mainly at the emotioning, the preferences of living that guide the flow of the systemic conservation through systemic reproduction of the manner of living conserved.

Beginnings

The study and comparison of human and chimpanzee genetic constitution shows two fundamental facts. One is that the human and the chimpanzee lineages must have become separated from a common origin some time between five and six million years ago. The other is that the comparison of human and chimpanzee nucleic acids shows that these differ by less than 2 percent. But, if the above is the case, how is it that chimpanzees and humans are such different kinds of animals? Yet we can easily see that we resemble chimpanzees in many respects. Can we learn about how we are as human beings by studying chimpanzees because our genetic constitution resembles theirs? Or can we learn about chimpanzees by studying humans because of this resemblance? Before going on with these questions, let us ask: "How do we humans and chimpanzees differ in our manners of living?"

In the early 1980's Frans de Waal published a book that he called *Chimpanzee Politics*, the outcome of a careful and prolonged study of a chimpanzee community of about twenty-five individuals, infants, juveniles and adults, males and females — kept in an enormous ground in a zoo in Arnheim, Holland. What Frans de Waal shows in his book, is that the inter-individual relations among adults in that chimpanzee community were mostly centered in a continuous and recurrent dynamics of domination and submission. Furthermore, he also shows that chimpanzees, whether in the big area occupied by this particular captive colony or in the wild, instrumentalize their relations by manipulating each other in the continuous struggle for domination and submission in which they live. No doubt the chimpanzee mother/child relations are relations of care, and the chimpanzee children are playful in their relations (and become more so as they associate with humans if these treat them lovingly), yet Frans de Waal's study shows that the basic or guiding mood of a chimpanzee community is that of an ongoing dynamics of competition in relations of domination and submission among the adults that spreads through all ages when an open conflict arises.

In choosing the title *Chimpanzee Politics*, Frans de Waal compares the behavior of the chimpanzees with human behavior in our Western culture. That he does so is made apparent when he quotes Aristotle saying that "man is a political animal," equating politics with the struggle for domination and submission in a community life, as if this were the natural human manner of co-existence, and as if this manner of coexistence were social living. For Aristotle, politics was living in the city with care for the affairs of the community of citizens, but now the word "politics" mostly means the struggle for power and control of the affairs of the city community. But it is with this latter connotation that Frans de Waal speaks of "chimpanzee politics" when comparing chimpanzee community life with human social life. We think differently from Frans de Waal in respect to human social life. We think that even though we modern human beings live greatly immersed in the dynamics of domination and submission, that is, in political struggle, we are not political animals. Indeed, we claim that human beings belong to an evolutionary history in which daily life was centered on cooperation and not on domination and submission. In other words, we claim that we human beings are not political animals because we belong to an evolutionary history in which the basic emotion or mood was love and not competition and aggression. This is a biological claim, not a philosophical one.

Not all animal relations are of the same kind because they take place in the relational dynamics of different emotions, and the emotion defines the character of the relations. Thus, we think that in the human domain, what we distinguish as work and political relations are relations of a different kind than social relations because they take place in different emotions than the emotion in which social relations take place. That this is so is apparent in our daily life, in that we expect others as well as ourselves to act or behave differently in work, political, or social relations. Thus, for example, in work relations we are in the emotion of obligation, in political relations we are in the emotion of mistrust and the desire for manipulation, whereas in social relations we are in the emotion of trust and mutual respect - that is, in love. Accordingly, we claim that the mood or emotion that constitutes social relations is love (Maturana and Verden-Zöller, 1993), and that love is the domain of those relational behaviors through which another arises as a legitimate other in co-existence with oneself.

Cooperation takes place in social relations, and not in relations of domination and submission. Social relations entail trust as well as the absence of manipulation or instrumentalization in the interpersonal relations. Indeed, social relations break down when manipulation appears. If one inquires among the members of a human community about their opinions concerning politics, one finds a fair number of persons who express their dislike of politics because they see it as a domain of manipulation and instrumentalization of human relations. In its Greek origin, politics had to do with a concern for the affairs of the community. No doubt this is still an element, but the attempt to assure a democracy, or some other desired organization of affairs, has repeatedly led to authoritative relations in which more and more instrumentalization and manipulation of human relations is accepted. Given this, Frans de Waal had no difficulty in choosing to call a book dealing with the relations of domination and submission among chimpanzees in their community life, Chimpanzee Politics.

From what Frans de Waal and others who have studied chimpanzee communities have shown, it is apparent that the basic emotion or background mood in which chimpanzee group life occurs is that proper to political life - namely, mistrust. Mistrust leads to a recurrent dynamic of manipulation of inter-individual relations which results in hidden aggressions and alliances in a struggle for domination and submission. We think, however, that what happens with us human beings is different from what happens with chimpanzees, notwithstanding that our present cultural life seems to be centered on the struggle for power, in a dynamics that is political exactly in the terms implied by Frans de Waal. And we think that what happens with us is different because the basic emotion or mood under which human community life occurs is that proper to a cooperative life - namely, love. We are saying that we think the fundament of human living is love, and that cooperation in humans arises through the pleasure of doing things together in mutual trust, not through the manipulation of relations. We do not say that love is the only emotion under which we human beings live. Of course not. Certainly, we human beings flow or can flow in our emotioning through all the emotional dimensions that we can live. But we claim that it can be argued biologically that we are the kind of beings that we are because love has been the emotion that has grounded the course of the evolutionary history that gave origin to us.

We human beings become ill at any age if we have to live a life centered in mistrust, instrumentalization, and manipulation of relations. Our children need to grow in trust, mutual care, body acceptance and cooperation, to become well-integrated individuals and social beings as they learn their bodies and the bodies of others in the generation of a social space (see Verden-Zöller in Maturana and Verden-Zöller, 1993).

How can the difference between the human and the chimpanzee manners of community living be explained and understood? How is it that chimpanzees did not become languaging animals like us? How can we explain the difference of intelligence between humans and chimpanzees? Before we propose an answer to these questions, we would like to remark that we do not think that we can learn about human beings studying chimpanzees, or vice versa. We think that the study of chimpanzees may expand our ability to see ourselves by opening a space for our reflections on our different manners of living. But at the same time, we think that the study of chimpanzees does not lead us to understand how is it that we humans are as we are, because we humans and chimpanzees are different kinds of animals, resulting from a different evolutionary history.

Neoteny

Animals in general, and mammals in particular, move in their relations between two extremes: one of mutual respect and mutual trust in total body acceptance in bodily nearness, and the other in a dynamics of relations of domination and submission. In mammals, the first manner of relating is usually confined to the mother/child relation and to the period of childhood or upbringing of the offspring, whereas the second is the usual manner of relation in adulthood, a period that begins in relation to the age of reproduction. The chimpanzees in their inter-individual relations in captive and wild communities resemble this standard pattern more than we human beings do. We think this indicates that the ancestor that we share with them cannot have been different from the usual mammalian form. How did the two lineages diverge?

Our proposition (and this is, of course, a speculative proposition), is that the two lineages that gave origin to us and to the chimpanzees diverged through the conservation of a different emphasis in the two basic mammalian manners of relating mentioned above. We humans are the present form, we think, of a lineage that arose defined and constituted by the conservation of the progressive expansion of the mother/child relation of mutual body acceptance, nearness, and mutual care in playfulness and total trust, in a manner that also involved the male, and progressively extended beyond the age of reproduction into the adult life in a neotenic evolutionary trend. And we think that the chimpanzees are the present of a lineage in which the whole basic mammalian pattern of inter-individual relations was mostly conserved, perhaps even in a manner that put more emphasis on the opposing relations of domination and submission along the adult life than the original one.

That we belong to a lineage, or system of lineages, with neotenic characteristics (characteristics that result from an evolutionary history of expansion of childhood beyond the period of reproduction) is, of course, well known to biologists. Indeed, biologists emphasize this by claiming that many of our human body features resemble those of chimpanzee children or babies more than those of adult chimpanzees. What we want to emphasize here now, though, is that this expansion of childhood into adulthood in the system of lineages that gave origin to us has entailed in a fundamental manner the expansion of the emotioning of the mother/child relation of mutual body acceptance and total trust into adulthood. And we also want to emphasize that the conservation of the expansion of the mother/child dynamics of love and play relations into the adult living has been the operational reference for all the body and relational changes that eventually constituted us as the kind of animals that we are as human beings.

We claim that it is as a result of this neotenic trend that we humans are cooperative animals dependent on love at all ages. The chimpanzee is not the present of a neotenic history and we think that the neoteny in the evolution of chimpanzees has not entailed the expansion of the emotioning of the mother/child relation as a central in the evolutionary shaping of their manner of living. On the contrary, the chimpanzee is, we think, the present of an evolutionary history in which adulthood has remained adulthood, or may even have been expanded into youth, as competition has been emphasized as a basic relational mood. It is chimpanzees who are in fact political animals, not us human beings.

Intelligence

If we reflect about the circumstances in daily life under which we speak of intelligence, we will notice that we do so when we refer to the consensual abilities of a human or non-human animal. Consensuality takes place as the spontaneous, coherent behavioral transformation of two or more organisms in a particular domain of coexistence as a result of their living together in recurrent and recursive interactions, and the behavioral domain that arises through consensuality is a consensual domain. Flexibility of behavior according to the circumstances of living with conservation of living is what an observer connotes when he or she speaks of intelligence, or, better, of intelligent behavior. The ability to behave adequately in a situation that an observer sees as a problem is what an observer calls problem solving. As such, problem solving is only a manner of talking by an observer about the operation of an organism in a consensual domain when he or she does not know whether the organism will behave or not behave according to what he or she considers adequate. The capacity for consensuality and plastic behavior to which we refer as we speak of intelligence differs according to the different manners of living of the different organisms. Different manners of living occur as different domains of operational structural coherences between organism and medium, and as such they entail different possibilities for intelligence as different domains of plastic behaviors.

In summary, when we speak of intelligence in daily life, we connote the capacity that an organism has to participate with others (or with the medium) in the constitution, expansion, and operation in a domain of consensual behaviors (or of plastic dynamic coherences) while under the continuous structural changes that it undergoes in its individual life (see Maturana and Guiloff, 1980). In these circumstances, what can we say about intelligence in the human and chimpanzee lineages? Let us have first an indirect approximation.

The fundamental difference between human beings and chimpanzees is not that we are rational animals and they are not. Of course we live in language and they do not. Although chimpanzees use many different sounds, movements, and gestures that an observer may recognize as operations in language as indicators of objects or of situations, their manner of living is not based in languaging. The fundamental difference, according to us, belongs to the different basic emotional dynamics (configuration of emotioning) conserved in our different lineages along our respective evolutionary histories as different manners of living that have resulted different bodyhoods and different manners of living. Different manners of living as languaging and not languaging beings characterize humans and chimpanzees as different kinds of animals. No doubt both lineages entail a history of expansion of the basic capacity of consensuality, and hence, of intelligence, but in one of them, in us, this expansion has taken place in a manner of living centered on cooperation, whereas in the other it has taken place in a manner of living centered on competition and the manipulation of relations. Yes, we human beings also can manipulate each other and in our modern patriarchal culture we do so, but our claim is that as we are cooperative animals, our evolutionary history could not have been centered on aggression and mutual manipulation.

Cooperation is a consensual activity that arises in a domain of mutual acceptance in a co-participation that is invited, not demanded. The basic grounding emotion or mood in cooperation is love, and as cooperation takes place in the pleasure of mutual acceptance, its realization occurs in play (see Maturana and Verden-Zöller, 1993), in the enjoyment of actually doing things together. As cooperation entails the pleasure of doing with the other, it is open to continuous expansion in the domain in which it takes place. In a life centered in trust, cooperation, and mutual acceptance - that is, in love, the opening for consensuality is multidimensional, and, in fact, unlimited. In mutual acceptance and in mutual trust, all situations of life become opportunities for the pleasure of doing things together - that is, for cooperation.

The conservation of a manner of living centered in cooperation constitutes an opportunity for an unlimited and unrestricted systemic expansion of intelligence as a recursive evolutionary opening for the continuous generation of new domains of consensuality and their extension. Such expansion of intelligence also occurs in the ontogeny of individuals living in cooperation. The conservation of a manner of living immersed in competition and in the struggle for domination and submission does not negate consensuality altogether, but restricts its scope to a narrow path of coexistence in struggle and competition which, in essence, is always the same - mutual negation.

We now re-consider the question of the origin of humanness.

Humanness

When did humanness begin? We have claimed that we humans exist in language, or, more precisely, that we exist in conversations that are the braiding of languaging and emotioning. And we also maintain that humanness arose when in a lineage of bipedal primates the living in conversations began to be conserved generation after generation in the learning of the children as the manner of living that constituted and defined that lineage. When did that happen? We think that happened - and humanness began — not later than about three and a half million years ago, and we propose that it happened in the following manner.

Some 3,300,000 years ago, some small bipedal primates *(Australopithecus afarensis)* lived in Africa, in the north of what is now Kenya. Their height was about the height of an 8 year-old child. Judging by their body anatomy and their teeth, these primates could have been our ancestors, or very similar to them (see Johanson and Maitland, 1981, and Johanson and Shreeve, 1989). The common ancestor that we share with chimpanzees was not bipedal, but their descendants in our lineage must have become so as they became ground dwellers in the savannahs at the fringe of the forests, as they moved, conserving from generation to generation the habit of moving erect as they looked around while moving among the tall grasses. We belong to a system of lineages of primates that as ground dwellers became bipedal, whereas chimpanzees belong to a system of lineages that remained quadrupedal on the ground.

The bipedal primates of somewhat more than 3 million years ago were not hunters, or if they did hunt occasionally, their prey must have been small animals. Their teeth, very similar to ours, were those of gatherers who eat seeds, nuts, roots, insects, and the remains of animals killed by large predators. Furthermore, paleontological findings indicate that these primates lived in small groups of some five to eight individuals of both sexes and of all ages. Their brains were about a third the size of ours now, and their faces were different, more like that of a young chimpanzee.

Their hands, however, were like our hands in that they had fingers that could be fully extended and opposed to the thumb. No doubt, judging by their manner of existing as gatherers, they were capable of complex and delicate visual and finger correlations in the handling of food. But human hands are much more than instruments for manipulation - indeed, they are caressing organs. The fingers of the human hand can be extended fully as well as delicately flexed, allowing the hand as a totality to accommodate to any curved surface of the body in a caressing touch, more or less in the same manner that the tongue of other animals does. In modern human beings, hand caresses occupy the whole hand with the fingers flexing adequately to fit the caressed surface in a gentle holding touch. The hand of the chimpanzee does not do so easily because the fingers cannot be totally extended. The hand of our ancestors 3 million years ago, although not identical in its proportions to ours now, had all the characteristics of a human hand, both as a manipulating and as a caressing organ.

Let us now reconstruct the possible manner of living of our ancestors 3.3 million years ago from what we know of *Australopithecus afarensis* as if our ancestors were very similar to them, and compare it with our present manner of living.

1. Judging by their teeth and their size, our ancestors must have lived as gatherers, eating seeds, roots, nuts, insects, small vertebrates, and occasionally scavenging the remains of big animals killed by large predators.

    We modern human beings are still gatherers of seeds, nuts, roots, and fruits. Indeed, agriculture is a way of remaining a gatherer. That we are gatherers is shown also in the success of supermarkets, and in the fact that in situations of need we easily resort to gathering, and even scavenging.

2. Paleontological remains indicate that our ancestors lived in small groups of about five to eight individuals of all ages.

    We modern human beings feel comfortable in families of that size, and even when we form larger communities, we live in intimacy in small groups.

3. Our ancestors may have shared food as a feature of their manner of living. Food sharing takes place in the direct passing of food from one individual to another. This is not a very rare phenomenon - many animals such as birds and ants do it as a central aspect of their manner of living, but it is not common among primates. Many parent birds feed their children by depositing the food directly into their mouths. In a

neotenic lineage like ours, this practice may have been a feature of the mother/child relations conserved into the post-reproductive stage as part of the trend of neotenic expansion of our lineage, and is still present in the pleasure of a mouth to mouth kiss.

We modern humans share food. In some cultures women frequently pass what they are chewing directly from their mouth to the mouths of their babies, or to the mouths of old people who have lost their teeth. Our children often take food from their mouths to give it to an adult or to another child. Our food-sharing behavior is not cultural. That this is so is apparent in the just mentioned spontaneous food sharing of our little children—we have the biology of sharing animals.

Our genetic constitution (our biological primary structure) does not determine what happens in us in our lifetime as individuals, because whatever happens does so in an epigenetic manner in a historical process of interactions between organism and medium. But nothing can happen in the course of our epigenesis that our genetic constitution does not permit as a possible feature of our ontogeny. We are sharing animals now; therefore, we belong to an evolutionary history that conserved food sharing as a manner of living. We do not know when this history began, but we believe that it must have been already established in our ancestors of 3 million years ago in all ages as part of the evolutionary neotenic trend of their lineage.

4. We suppose that among our ancestors of 3 million years ago, males participated in child care through loving relations in the pleasure of living together. In what manner, we do not know; perhaps playing with the children in body contact, carrying them, feeding or sharing food with them, as well as being attentive to their play without restricting them. Male gibbons nowadays do so as they participate with the females in the care of their offspring.

We modern human males care for our children in the manner described above, and we do so with natural ease and spontaneous pleasure when there are no cultural injunctions to the contrary in terms of control and instrumentalization through the demand for obedience. We think that the emotional dynamic that brings human males to participate in child care is also an evolutionarily conserved feature of our neotenic trend, not a new cultural one. As such, male child care is an epigenic behavior that can be fostered or repressed. Adult male care for children in the pleasure of playing with them, is not very frequent in primates, but it sometimes occurs as a juvenile behavior, as can occasionally be seen in a zoo.

5. We modern human beings are sensual and tender animals. We caress each other, we enjoy body nearness and contact. Caresses evoke in us physiological well-being. We caress each other not only with actual touches, but also with words, with the tone of our voices, with our regard, or with what we do. All these caresses evoke in us physiological changes that constitute well-being. In us the hand is, so to speak, a caressing organ, and the touch of the hand is physiologically healing. But not only that, we enjoy all sensorial dimensions as sources of pleasure and well-being, as features of what can be called the aesthetics of living.

We do not know how our ancestors behaved, but we can assume that as primates who possessed a caressing hand, and as members of a neotenic lineage, they were also sensual and tender animals that, like us, lived in the conservation of the relational configurations of caresses and mutual care in both adulthood and youth. We also think that such basic extended sensuality, with the sensorial curiosity that it brings, is part of the neotenic trend of our lineage through the conservation of the expanded sensuality involved in the extension of childhood.

As we look at this speculative but plausible reconstruction of the relational features of the life of our ancestors of over 3 million years ago and compare it with our own in the present (neglecting the particularities of how we do what we do), we discover that our manner of living and theirs must have been the same, save in one respect - namely, language and the features of the body associated with it. If our ancestors were as we suggest, how did language arise?

Humanness and Languaging

To the extent that language is a manner of living in coordinations of coordinations of consensual behaviors, nearness of co-existence in doing many things together is necessary for language to arise. At the same time, for nearness of co-existence to occur as a relational background in which languaging could arise spontaneously in the recursion of doing things together, it must be permanent, or recurrent and sufficiently prolonged. What can we say now about what may have been the biological fundaments for such nearness in the origin of our lineage as languaging primates?

Judging by the brain capacity of the skull of *Australopithecus afarensis* (about 450 cc), the brain of our ancestors 3 million years ago must have been larger than the brain of a domestic dog. Indeed, it must have been about the size of the brain of a chimpanzee. Dogs do not live in language among themselves or with us, but when we live with them in some stable nearness in intimacy and in the proper flow of recurrent interactions, we can live languaging circumstances with them, in which they participate in a more or less extended episodic manner. So the brain size of a dog allows it to enter with us in consensual coordinations of consensual coordinations of behaviors.

But for that to happen to a dog living with us, or for that to happen between any pair of animals, certain emotioning (or configuration of relational dynamics) is necessary. That is, the emotioning must be such that the frequent and recurrent interactions that take place between those animals should constitute a domain of coordinations of behavior in which recursive consensual coordinations of coordinations of behavior may arise. Furthermore, a special emotioning must also take place in the living together in coordinations of consensual behaviors so that the occasional episodes of languaging lived may become a manner of living that is conserved as a matter of course in the spontaneous learning of the offspring, with the result that a lineage defined by a coexistence in language begins. According to us, since *love* is the only emotional dynamics that gives rise to a living together in the close and sensual nearness in which a prolonged living together in recursive consensual coordinations of doings can take place for the pleasure of it, *that emotioning must be love.*

What we in fact propose is that languaging must have begun as a manner of living that has been conserved generation after generation in the spontaneous learning of children more than 3 million years ago, and we think that it began among our ancestors as a simple result of their living together in small groups as gatherers who shared food in love in the intimacy of tenderness and sensuality. Moreover, we maintain that living in languaging arose not because it was necessary, or in any way advantageous, but merely as a result of this manner of living together. Certainly, we do not mean that there were not occasions of dispute or of anger and quarrel, but we claim that aggression and mistrust cannot have been the basic mood of co-existence in our ancestors. And we claim so because if that had been the case, the manner of living in recursive consensual coordinations of behavior that living in language is could not have arisen, because there would not have been the space of intimate and stable cooperative coexistence that makes such a living possible.

Why do we think that languaging as a manner of living should have begun at least 3 million years ago and not later? Simply because of the number of generations that we think was required for the establishment and conservation of an epigenic dynamics that produced and secured through genetic co-option the conservation of all the anatomical and physiological changes associated with languaging as we now live it in speech.

Languaging as a manner of daily living in consensual coordinations of consensual coordinations of behavior can in fact take place in many different manners. In us, languaging takes place mostly through speech, so it must have involved sound production by mouth in correlation with coordinations of behavior from very early in this history. Let us recall that a lineage begins in the recursive reproductive conservation of a manner of living; let us also recall that the reproductive conservation of a manner of living is systemic and not genetically determined, even though it entails the systemic conservation of the genetic constitution of the initial organic structure that makes possible the epigenetic realization of the manner of living conserved. To reformulate in dynamic terms what we have just said:

Due to the systemic nature of the phenomena of reproduction and heredity, two intertwined processes take place in the establishment and conservation of a lineage:

1. The genetic changes that take place along the history of a lineage become continuously co-opted into the realization and conservation of the manner of living (ontogenic phenotype) that defines the lineage, and follow a general course channeled as a historical trend of genetic change by the systemic realization and conservation of that manner of living.

2. At the same time, a lineage is conserved only as long as the genetic conditions and the conditions of the medium that permit the realization of the epigenetic course that makes possible the realization of the manner of living that defines it, are conserved systemically generation after generation.

There is no doubt that the systemic conservation of the manner of living that defines a lineage requires a structural fundament in the organism and in the medium. In the organism this fundament is a genetic constitution that makes it possible that the individual members of the lineage may realize in their epigenesis the manner of living of the lineage while sliding through a medium - conserving organization and adaptation as long as the medium, that is also arising and changing with them, has the structure that permits that to happen. Furthermore, the possibility that the offspring of a lineage may give origin at any particular historical moment to a new manner of living as a variation on the manner of living of their parents, arises in the epigenetic interplay of the independent structural variabilities of the new organisms and the circumstances of the medium in which they happen to be at that particular historical moment (see Appendices 2 and 3). In other words, the reproductive conservation of a manner of living involves the conservation of both the genetic constitution and the features of the medium that make it possible. That is, and we repeat because this is a basic notion, the reproductive conservation generation after generation of a manner of living does not occur as a genetically determined process precisely because the manner of living conserved in a lineage arises epigenetically. And this happens when the particular configuration of dynamic relations between an organism and the medium that constitutes the epigenetic realization of the manner of living conserved repeats generation after generation through the realization of that very same manner of living. Such is, of course, the systemic dynamics of reproductive conservation of an ontogenic phenotype, or manner of living.

In summary, the reproduction of an organic identity entails the reproduction of both the genetic constitution and the medium that makes possible its epigenetic realization. In general terms: when, in the ecological history of the biosphere, conditions arise in the interplay between organisms and medium for the epigenetic realization of a new manner of living in the successive reproduction of some organisms, and the new manner of living begins to be reproductively conserved systemically, a new lineage arises. Such a lineage lasts as long as the relation between the changing genetic conditions of the organisms and the changing structure of the medium remains such that the systemic conditions that make possible the realization of the ontogenic phenotype of the lineage are conserved. In that process, organism and medium change together congruently as integral coherent systemic components of a changing biosphere.

When such a systemic process happens, the manner of living systemically conserved generation after generation necessarily co-opts in its structural dynamics any variation (genetically and otherwise) compatible with the realization of the manner of living conserved. Furthermore, as a lineage is established, a trend arises as a systemic constraint for the diversification of the future lineages as an operational canalization for the genetic and non-genetic variations that may be conserved. Such a process is a historical process, and as such has a unidirectionality that in living systems always entails the conservation of a constellation of coherent changes that go together through many generations. One can say that the ontogenic phenotype conserved in a lineage canalizes the genetic drift of the lineage in a dynamics of recursive co-option of all genetic variations that do not deny it.

We think that this must have happened in our evolutionary history in relation to the changes that have taken place in the brain, in the larynx, in the face, in the respiratory dynamics, in the structure of the neck, and so forth, of our ancestors, as well as in their manner of living together, while their being speech languaging animals became systemically conserved generation after generation through their living as speech-languaging animals. That is, according to us, such changes and transformation must have been the result of an evolutionary trend constituted by the conservation of a manner of living in conversations through sound productions in a background of intimacy in the biology of love. Furthermore, we think that the transformation of the bodyhood of our ancestors into our present integrated bodyhood of languaging humans, cannot have taken place in a few generations. The greatest part of the genetic system (95% or more, perhaps,) is involved in the regulatory dynamics of epigenesis, and thus its operation is open in each organism to a continuous epigenic modulation by the flow of the systemic realization of its ontogenic phenotype. As a result, most genetic changes in a lineage, which necessarily must affect the domain of the regulatory dynamics, are open to be systemically co-opted for the conservation or change of the manner of living that defines the lineage. Accordingly, we think that this is how the genetic change follows the conservation of the ontogenic phenotype, and not the reverse. Finally, it is because we think that the continuous accommodation of the genetic system to the systemic conservation of a manner of living is a process that involves genetic co-option in the domain of genetic regulation of the epigenesis of morphogenesis, that we think that our history of languaging primates must be of at least 3 million years (perhaps more than some 300,000 generations).

Reproduction and Heredity

The question about genetic (DNA) or non-genetic determination of the phenomenon of heredity is not a trivial one. Our claim is that the phenomenon of heredity is a systemic rather than a genetic or molecular one. We do not deny the participation of DNA in giving long-run stability to biological phenomena and lineages as well as in determining the range of possible variations in the epigenetic process. Nothing can happen in the life history of an organism that is not permitted or made possibly by its genetic constitution, but at the same time nothing is determined (or, more precisely, predetermined) in the life history of an organism by its genetic constitution, because every feature in it arises in an epigenic process. Furthermore, as all biologists know, the phenotype obscures the genotype in the epigenetic process because, in fact, many different genotypes can give rise to the same ontogenic phenotype. However, not all biologists are fully aware that epigenesis is a systemic process of mutual structural modulation that involves both the organism and the medium over the life span of the organism. And we biologists are not always aware of this because in our modern inclination to reductionistic thinking, we frequently see the organism as if it were interacting with a pre-existing and already specified medium that contains it, or we make it disappear altogether in the enhancement of the genes.

The fundamental point in what we say here is our claim that the characteristics of an organism arise in a systemic dynamics through the recurrent and recursive interactions of the organism and the medium, in a process in which both the organism and the medium change together congruently, and not in a manner caused or predetermined by the genetic constitution of the organism or by the structure of the medium. Accordingly, we claim that:

1. Heredity occurs as a systemic process;
2. The process of evolution follows a course led by the systemic conservation of changes in the manner of living or the organisms, and not a course led by the genetic variations, even though these are always involved;
3. Evolutionary genetic change occurs as a genetic drift, and the course of the genetic drift in a lineage is channeled by the systemic conservation of the manner of living that defines the lineage; and
4. The systemic conservation of a manner of living co-opts any genetic and epigenetic variation that does not interfere with it.

Thus, evolution as a process of constitution, diversification, and extinction of lineages is not a process of improvement of the manner of living, or of progress in any particular or general sense, but it is a continuous changing present that arises in the continuous systemic conservation of the realization of the living. In evolution nothing happens because it is necessary, advantageous, or desirable. Indeed, a particular epigenic course until then optional in a lineage that begins to be systemically conserved as a manner of living in a new lineage, may become not optional but necessary in the conservation of the constitution of the new lineage through genetic constraints after several generations only to the extent that the manner of living conserved may have channeled the genetic drift of the lineage and the changes of the medium in the facilitation of the realization of that manner of living. As a result, after a certain number of generations, nothing of the medium or of the manner of living that defines the new lineage can be easily removed or altered without destroying the organisms of the lineage. Such alterations would destroy or distort the systemic coherences of the realization of the organisms that had been established along the history of the lineage. In other words, it is because of the systemic coherent changes that occur in the organism and medium in the evolutionary process, that it appears to a casual observer as if the features that define a lineage had initially arisen because they were necessary, or because they constituted an improvement for the survival of the members of the lineage.

Thus, although languaging is now essential for human existence because it now constitutes human existence in a medium that has arisen through languaging, languaging did not arise, nor was it conserved, because it was initially in any sense necessary for the survival of our ancestors. Episodes of languaging must have been happening first occasionally and then frequently in the predecessors of our lineage, until languaging began to be conserved as a matter of course in the learning of their children in a systemic inheritance. When that happened, a new manner of living and a whole new system of lineages began in a process that co-opted all genetic variations in the conservation of living in language through living in languaging. Languaging now seems essential to us, and it is in fact essential for our human living, because everything has changed in our lives around the systemic conservation of our living in language.

But how is it that living in language did not happen in the chimpanzee lineage? How is it that our ancestors lived as they lived, and languaging arose and was conserved as a manner of living? How was our lineage established in the conservation of a life lived in conversations?

Biology of Trust and Nearness

Trust and nearness constitute intimacy as the fundament for doing things together in the pleasure of doing them with another. And doing things together in the pleasure of doing them with another, constitutes cooperation. Finally, intimacy — the pleasure and joy of trust and nearness in play in total mutual body acceptance — has its origin in the mother/child relation and its expansion in neoteny.

We humans belong to a neotenic lineage, a lineage defined by the transgenerational conservation of the progressive expansion of childhood characteristics into adulthood. As a result of this process, reproduction in us humans now takes place, so to say, in the middle of infancy. Yet as neoteny occurs in evolution, it is not infancy or childhood proper that is conserved or expanded. Rather, some features of the child's body development and emotional dynamics are extended, so that the tasks of the adult life are progressively realized in the members of the evolving lineage by individuals who retain more and more infantile relational characteristics.

We think that in us this process of neoteny entails the conservation into adulthood of the relational dynamics of love proper to the mother/child and to the child/child relations in the mammalian basic emotioning. Love, as we have said already, is the domain of those behaviors through which an other arises as a legitimate other in coexistence with oneself. Love means or entails mutual trust in total body acceptance with no manipulation or instrumentalization of the relations. These relational features are central in the mother/child relation. Manipulation and instrumentalization of another are attempts to control the behavior of the other by illegitimate means; they are manners of aggression and denial of the other and thus entail a different emotion than love. And when the manipulated being becomes emotionally aware of this, mistrust and anger arise.

Modern human beings are love dependent animals at all ages, and we think that this is so because love as a feature of adult life has been conserved in our lineage as a neotenic feature. Of course, we do not say that we humans are unique in being loving animals. Certainly not. Indeed, mammals in general are loving animals at their infancy, and we humans in our loving behavior can relate and evoke loving behavior practically with all vertebrates, at least during their childhood, but also in their adulthood. What we say is that we are peculiar in that our evolutionary history is centered in the biology of love as a basic feature of our manner of living in a way that has expanded through our whole life span. But we think that there is more.

We think that in the conservation and expansion of the emotioning of the mother/child relation in the neotenic history of our lineage, and prior to the beginning of the conservation of language as a manner of living, there was a transformation of sexuality in our female ancestors. In the course of this history, the short annual period of female desire for and enjoyment of body contact and sexual intercourse expanded and became continuous. At what historical moment did this happen? We do not know, but we think that its happening had a fundamental consequence that made the origin of language and its conservation as a manner of living possible. Such a happening separated sexual intercourse from reproduction for our ancestors, allowing sex as the domain of acceptance and enjoyment of body contact in general, and genital intercourse in particular, to operate as an expanded source of pleasure and stability in the formation of interpersonal relations, particularly in couples and small families.

Sexuality as a source of joy and pleasure in the nearness of the body of a particular other gives permanence to the close relations between the members of a couple or of a small group. And as the expansion of the female sexuality expands the joy of nearness, it creates a possibility for the enjoyment of doing things together in the pleasure of mutual acceptance through the conservation of that nearness. Accordingly, we think that the expansion of female sexuality as part of the neotenic trend of our lineage created a space of stable intimacy, pleasure, and trust around her, in a dynamics of mutual acceptance and enjoyment of recurrent body contact that drew together females, males, and children in small families of a cooperative living together.

Sexuality does not entail only sexual intercourse; it includes, in greater or lesser degrees, all aspects of body acceptance in total trust and in the enjoyment of body nearness and contact, regardless of the sex of the participants. Thus, sexuality is involved in platonic friendship, in friendly embraces, in the acceptance and enjoyment of the nearness of another, implying in each situation different dimensions of body mutual acceptance in nearness and contact than those involved in genital sexual coupling, regardless of whether these are heterosexual or homosexual. Accordingly, what we say is that the expansion of the sexuality of the females of our ancestors is peculiar because as it occurred, and the females became as continuously interested and desirous of sexual nearness and genital intercourse as the males, a domain of coexistence appeared in which living together in small intimate groups became a permanent source of pleasure, of joy in the company of the other, and of playfulness around the realization of the chores of daily life in cooperation and not in competition.

Neoteny entails also the expansion beyond the reproductive age into adulthood of features of the mother/child relation such as sensuality and tenderness. Sensuality entails sensorial expansion and openness to see, touch, hear, smell, whereas tenderness has to do with the behavior of care in relation to others, a typical although not exclusive mammalian mother/child behavioral feature. A mammalian mother (and in fact, all animal adults when they care for their offspring) senses more when with children. This is easily observable in a female cat with kittens as she is ready to see, hear, touch and smell what she would not see, hear, touch, or smell, if she were not mothering. A female cat with kittens is also ready to protect her kittens, to let them climb on her body, or to lie on the ground so that the kittens can nurse. When one sees these behaviors, one easily says that the cat is behaving with tenderness. The same is obviously apparent in a hen with chicks. This emotional appreciation is not a projection of our own emotioning; it is a distinction of the relational domain in which these animals are.

We claim that the neotenic trend in our lineage resulted in an expansion of the mother/child relations of body acceptance, sensuality and tenderness into the adulthood of our ancestors as relational features of their daily life. And we also claim that those features have been conserved in our lineage, and are still present in us in our daily behavior at all ages, unless we deny them specifically through some ad hoc rational argument, or through some mishandling of the emotional upbringing of our children. Furthermore, we think, as we said above, that the expansion of female sexuality as part of the conservation of the neotenic trend in our lineage resulted in the intertwining of sensuality, tenderness, and sexuality that gave, and still gives, stability to family coexistence. The expansion of female sexuality constituted the joy in doing things together in cooperation as a manner of living cultivated and conserved generation after generation in the learning of children.

Cooperation is doing things together in love, in trust and mutual acceptance, in the pleasure of the doing together. As such cooperation constitutes a relational space completely different from that in which relations of domination, submission and competition, take place. In other words, we use the word "cooperation" in daily life to refer to doing things together for an explicit or implicit common purpose in a space of full behavioral freedom, in trust, and in implicit or explicit mutual acceptance. Cooperation does not take place in a space of demands, mistrust, and control. Moreover, cooperation constitutes a relational space in which intelligence is spontaneously opened to continuous expansion without effort, as a simple result of love as the very emotioning that makes it possible as a manner of living. Finally, we think that it is only in the relational space of intimacy, in the acceptance of the body nearness of the other in cooperation, where living in language could arise, and in fact arose. Language could only arise in such a relational space, because it is only closeness in mutual acceptance and intimacy that makes it possible for occasional coordinations of consensual coordinations of behavior to begin to be conserved as a manner of living together. And we think that such a space of stable intimacy in love and cooperation was created in our lineage by the expansion of the sexuality of the females, as it opened a space for the expansion of sexuality in general.

Furthermore, we think that as the sexuality of the female expanded within the neotenic trend of the lineage, the sexuality of the male expanded as well in the domains of tenderness and sensuality, and female and male became co-participants in these dimensions. Male and female constituted each other in sensuality, tenderness and sexuality through participating in sensuality, tenderness, and sexuality. In this process they became systemic partners in living in cooperation, each one becoming a systemic participant in the conservation of sexuality as a source of pleasure and playfulness with the other (playfulness as the joy of doing in the joy living, see Maturana and Verden-Zöller, 1993). Indeed, we think that it must have been male/female playfulness in the neotenic trend that permitted and conserved the progressive expansion of female sexuality that made living in language possible. These are not romantic claims; it is enough to observe ourselves in our relations of friendship to see love undistorted by cultural injunctions or recommendations.

In the lineage that gave origin to the chimpanzees, things must have been different precisely because there was little expansion of neoteny after their lineage and ours separated some 6 million years ago, or because neoteny did not become the trend that defined their lineage. And we think that due to the absence of a neotenic trend there was not an expansion of the mother/child love relation into adulthood. Furthermore, we also think that due to the absence of such a neotenic trend, as well as due to the conservation of intense relations of domination and submission in the adult life of the members of the lineage that gave origin to chimpanzees, the members of that lineage never developed in their living together the degree of intimacy and permanence of the interpersonal relations in a coexistence that would have made it possible for them to live in cooperation and eventually to fully adopt languaging as a manner of living. When Frans de Waal talks in his writings about "chimpanzee politics," he directly refers to the life of chimpanzees as a manner of living centered in the struggle for domination and submission. In summary, we think that as chimpanzee remained political animals centered in the struggle for domination and submission in their adult life, they could not live enough recursive intimacy for languaging and living in conversations to become their manner of living.

Cooperative versus Political Living

We consider that we human beings are cooperative, not political animals, and we think so because cooperation is a central feature of the human manner of living. According to Frans de Waal and other observers, chimpanzees cooperate in aggression. Of course, operational mutual trust is basic for doing things together in aggression, and cooperation in aggression lasts as long as operational mutual trust lasts. But when mutual trust is not the fundamental mood that guides coexistence, cooperation is necessarily transitory, and doing things together becomes a feature of the political dynamics of the relations founded on circumstantial alliances, constituting a background of hypocrisy, as happens with chimpanzees.

We humans, of course, also participate in political alliances, but, we claim, not as a feature proper to the manner of living that made us humans. We think that political alliances have become a central feature of our cultural living in our European tradition only during the last 10,000 years since the origin of patriarchy. Indeed, we humans make political alliances fully aware that they are essentially transitory and not trustful because they are manipulative of the interpersonal relations as they occur outside love. That is, we know as we make them that coordinated actions based on political alliances, or any alliances based on coincidence of interests, are in themselves transitory and not to be trusted precisely because they are not based on love. Alliances do not have the permanence of a mutual acceptance rooted in a social manner of living, and they are not social actions, they are political actions. Thus, although we humans make political alliances, political alliances are not our fundamental form of coexistence. In us cooperation as a manner of living is essentially a daily life feature of a coexistence constituted on a basis of permanent mutual trust that stands on the conservation of love as the fundament for social living.

Intelligence and Cooperation

In our present patriarchal culture one usually speaks of intelligence in technical and professional domains as consisting of the ability to solve problems. Similarly, one speaks of cooperation as if it consisted of synergistic activities, regardless of the emotions involved. We, the authors, think differently. We think that if we attend to how we use the word intelligence in daily non-professional life, we see that we use it to refer to situations or circumstances in which a human or a non-human animal participates in a domain of consensual behaviors, either in one already established, or in the constitution of a new one. Thus, for example, if you take a kitten to your home, and you see that she easily learns where to deposit her feces, where you give her food, and how to sleep with you, you would probably say that she is very intelligent. The same would be true with a person.

With the word "cooperation" there is also a difference in its use in daily life and in more technical circumstances. In daily life we use the word "cooperation" in a manner that implies the emotioning of mutual acceptance and pleasure in doing things together, and not merely a coincidence of activity for increased effectiveness. It is in the way we use the words "intelligence" and "cooperation" in daily life, that we use these words in the present essay.

As we have said earlier, both political and cooperative living entail consensuality, but they do so differently. In a daily life lived as a political coexistence there is a restriction of attention to the domain of the struggle for domination and submission. This restriction of attention to competition in any circumstance constitutes a systemic dynamics that channels the possibility for the evolutionary expansion of intelligence into a narrow path. Cooperative coexistence, on the contrary, expands the attention of those that live together in it to all possible domains of coexistence in self respect and mutual acceptance. Thus, cooperation constitutes a systemic daily dynamics that is the foundation for a systemic evolutionary trend of expansion and conservation of intelligence. Let us not forget that emotions are lived in their realization and constitute systemic dynamics for their conservation.

The difference in brain size between chimpanzees (around 450 cc) and humans (around 1500 cc), with all the inner differences that such difference entails, is, according to us, the result of these two basically different manners of community living. One, the human manner of living, is fundamentally social in the conservation of cooperation and consensuality without restrictions, and constitutes the basis for an evolutionary trend of systemic expansion of intelligence during the whole life span. The other, the chimpanzee manner of living, is fundamentally political in the conservation of competition and the struggle for domination and submission, and constitutes the basis for an evolutionary trend of systemic restriction of intelligence to the narrow domain possible in competition in adult life. So, we think that the increase in brain size in the evolutionary history of our lineage is the consequence of the systemic reproductive conservation of a manner of living in cooperation rather than in competition and aggression. We modern human beings have a languaging, loving, and cooperative brain, so to speak, because we belong to a lineage in which languaging, cooperation, and love were systemically conserved in an evolutionary trend in which all genetic variations were systemically co-opted in the conservation and expansion of that manner of living.

Conservation of the Human Lineage

We think that the expansion of female sexuality in association with the neotenic trend of the human lineage has been fundamental for the constitution of the small cooperative groups or small families in which languaging arose and began to be conserved spontaneously, generation after generation, as a manner of living in the learning of the children as they lived in intimate sensuality, tenderness, and care.

Sexuality, tenderness, and sensuality, constituted in our origin and still constitute today, the fundamental relational dimensions on which rests the permanence of a family as a space of living together in cooperation and consensuality (see Appendix 7).

As we have indicated in another section of this essay, it is by the unidirectional restriction of viable variability brought about by the systemic conservation of a manner of living that a trend arises in the conservation of genetic and non-genetic changes in a lineage, or in a system of lineages. This is apparent in the transformation of the bodies of the members of our lineage in relation to the conservation of the human manner of living that began with the living in languaging. It is also apparent in the transformation of the baby's and mother's bodies under the conservation of the spontaneous sensual, tender, and playful behavior of the mother and baby in the joy of mutual touching and caressing. Accordingly, we think that the present form of the human body (its physiology, its anatomy, its genetics, and the emotional dynamics that come with these) is the result of an uninterrupted evolutionary history of coherent successive changes that have occurred in an uninterrupted trend defined by the conservation of a manner of living in conversations of tenderness and mutual care that channeled the genetic drift of the lineage. Moreover, we also think that this must have occurred as a feature of the phylogenic drift of a single family, or in a small network of inbreeding families. In such a history, the expansion of female sexuality must have created the intimacy and the fundament for the dynamics of systemic conservation of a close and permanent living together in an enjoyable coexistence that made possible both the living together in language and cooperation and the expansion of intelligence in the expansion of cooperative consensuality. No doubt that from the perspective of our present cultural living in a culture of domination and submission, mistrust and control, aggression, competition, political manipulations, abuse and wars, the claim that we modern human beings are the present of a biological history centered in love, trust, and cooperation seems preposterous and definitively wrong. And it seems so because we usually look at all biological process as if they had to take place according to our cultural emotioning. But if we look at the basic emotioning that brings joy and happiness in healthy human beings, we find love in its simplicity as the domain of those relational behaviors through which another arises as a legitimate other in coexistence with us.

There is no doubt that in the history of the *Homo* lineage to which we modern human beings belong, many branches must have arisen as variations around the conservation of a living in language that have taken a different course than ours. The fact that those lineages became extinct does not alter the validity of what we say, but it reveals that they went in different evolutionary courses than our lineage through the systemic conservation, perhaps, of conversations that did not conserve the biology of love and intimacy. We say this because we think that it is the conservation of living in language in the biology of love and intimacy that made us human beings.

In other words, we think that what was central in the constitution and survival of the primate lineage that resulted in humanity as we live it now was the conservation of love as the grounding emotion for coexistence in small family groups. This is why we think that the proper denomination of our Homo lineage from its beginning in the conservation of living in language to the present that we now live, should be *Homo sapiens-amans* (Bunnell, 1997). In this denomination the expression *sapiens* refers to living in language, and the expression *amans* refers to the basic emotion under which the lineage has been conserved. And we write *Homo sapiens-amans*, binding *sapiens* and *amans* with a hyphen, because we think that in the human origin languaging and emotioning were connected; love was the emotion that made possible the space of intimacy and permanence in living in the pleasure of doing things together in which languaging could arise as a manner of living conserved from generation to generation in the learning of the children.

Once living in language had begun to be conserved in our *Homo sapiens-amans* lineage, it became possible for other languaging lineages in which love progressively diminished its presence as a basic emotion to branch off from it. We think that initially those lineages did not and could not persist for long precisely because as love as the grounding emotion of daily living diminished in them, the group was unable to survive ecological disasters. The members of those lineages could not form stable communities with the kind of inner emotional coherence that could lead to the expansion and conservation of the intuition and understanding that result in the necessary cooperation to overcome such disasters.

Yet, when in the course of the evolutionary history our lineage of *Homo sapiens-amans* reached an expanded capacity for the manipulation of nature and for the argumentative justification, denial, or hiding of sentiments, other emotions such as arrogance and aggression could begin to be successfully conserved in daily living. When arrogance or aggression occurred occasionally, without being conserved from generation to generation in the learning of the children, its happening was historically irrelevant for the conservation of our condition as loving human beings. However we think that due to some particular circumstance of daily living in our ancestors some twelve thousand years ago, arrogance and aggression began to be nurtured in the learning of the children and became systematically conserved from one generation to the next as a manner of living. As that happened the relational dynamics entailed by these emotions replaced love as the relational grounding of group coexistence thus giving rise to a new cultural lineage centered on mistrust, control, domination and submission, appropriation and discrimination; namely the patriarchal culture that most humanity lives today

No doubt there are similarities between our behavior and the behavior of chimpanzees, and some of these similarities clearly correspond to primate features conserved in both of us from our common ancestors. However, other similarities, such as current political living, we think, are a recent (about 10,000 years, perhaps, in our European history) result of a cultural approach in our daily living as patriarchal beings to the political manner of living of the chimpanzees, which has a much longer biological history (4 or 5 million years, perhaps) of conservation of the struggle for domination and submission in adult life. Indeed, in the last seven or more thousand years of history in central Europe, life has progressively become more and more political through the increasing instrumentalization of all relations that our patriarchal coexistence in the dynamics domination, submission, and competition unavoidably brings forth (see the section on Patriarchy). What sort of consequences can this have in our biology? What consequences can this have in our physiology, anatomy, and genetics?

Ethics

Why and how is it that we modern human beings care about the consequences of our actions? Biology does not care. The cosmos does not care. We are the present of a cosmic and biological history that courses without aim, goal, or project. We have happened and nothing in the history that gave origin to us was necessary. We are a result of an evolutionary drift, not the product of a design or of a purpose. But as the kind of animals that we are as a result of such a history, we care, we have ethical concerns, we see our doings, and we care for their consequences to others or to the biosphere. According to us, this is so because we are loving animals. Love is not good or bad in itself, it is only the relational domain in which social life, trust, cooperation, and the expansion of intelligent behavior take place.

Ethical concerns, responsibility, and freedom, exist only in the domain of love as we live as languaging animals. Ethical concerns, responsibility, and freedom arise only as one sees the other and oneself, as well as the consequences of one's actions on the other or on oneself, and acts according to whether one wants or does not want those consequences. In other words, to have ethical concerns, to be responsible, to be free, one must see the other and oneself in his or her legitimacy. That is, one must operate as a languaging being in the biology of seeing the other as a legitimate other, which is the biology of love. Ethical concerns appear in the biosphere with human existence in language, and they either take place or not; if ethical concerns take place, ethical behaviors can take place.

Language is not a system of symbolic communications, language is a manner of living together in a flow of consensual coordinations of consensual coordinations of behaviors. Moreover, we do not just live in languaging, we live in conversations in the braiding of languaging and emotioning. Ethics is a particular kind of conversation, a reflexive conversation of seeing and care for the consequences of one's actions on others. In other words, ethics is a network of doings and emotioning in which the care and concern for the consequences of one's actions on others is present in what one does, and one acts in a way that entails accepting the consequences of that care and concern. Ethics belongs to the domain of emotions, not of reason, and as such it belongs to the domain of love.

We human beings care for other human beings and other living beings in the biosphere, and have ethical concerns and ethical behavior, because we are loving, languaging animals. That is, we belong to an evolutionary history in which the biology of love has been a central feature of the manner of living that defined our lineage. Yet, we see the other and care for him or her only to the extent that we have lived in the biology of love and intimacy, and have cultivated seeing and caring for the other as part of our living as caring human beings with other human beings. Moreover, it is as we live in recursive reflective conversations that allow us to look at our desires and see whether we like them or not in the context of other desires, that we can have ethical concerns and ethical behavior by caring for the consequences of our desires on others. That is, we belong to an evolutionary history in which living in language and in reflective conversations has been another central systemic feature of the manner of living that defined our lineage. Yet, it is only to the extent that we have lived in reflection by releasing our attachment to our desires, so that we become open to look at the consequences of what we do and act according to whether we like or do not like those consequences, that we can reflect on the consequences of our actions on others an thus have ethical concerns. Furthermore, to have ethical concerns we have to operate in respect for ourselves, accepting the legitimacy of our desires while releasing our attachment to them, so that we may reflect on the consequences of our actions and be responsible about them in the domain of our living with others without denying ourselves in the process. Yet, to do so we must live in self-respect and respect for the other, that is, in the biology of love.

We are not speaking of an ethical imperative. We are speaking of the biology of ethics, of what in our living as human beings makes our ethical concerns possible. We do not have to be ethical, but if we live in the biology of love as human beings, we sooner or later begin to have ethical concerns in relation to those other human beings whose living matters to us. We are not recommending love, nor are we recommending ethical behavior, but only if we live in the biology of love and have ethical concerns, can we indeed live as social human beings who do not become trapped in the culture of domination and submission or in the culture of indifference.

Love is our grounding, nearness our fundament, and when we lose love and nearness we try again and again to recover them because without them we disappear as *Homo sapiens-amans* even if our bodies may still remain *Homo sapiens* as zoological entities. Even health, our psychic and physiological health, depends on love and the acceptance of the body nearness of other human beings, and a word in love or a touch intended as a caress, may reestablish a lost physiological and psychic harmony. If we do not realize this, if we do not see that ethical concerns arise in love, and we believe that they belong to the domain of our rationality, in our desire for a harmonious social life we begin to use rational arguments or even force to secure something that looks like ethical behavior. As we lose respect for our emotions we begin to use rational arguments to hide, deny, or justify them. We do so in a path that progressively leads to the negation of the other through manipulation as we become *Homo sapiens aggressans* in the expansion of the patriarchal passion for control. We know all this, but we forget it in the delusion of omnipotence through a misunderstanding of intelligence as we think of it as an instrument of control and manipulation. But now that we are aware that our own behavior determines what we are and what our children become, we can choose: do we prefer to conserve a lineage of *Homo sapiens-amans* or a lineage of *Homo sapiens aggressans*? (See also Bunnell 1997, Bunnell and Sonntag, 2000.) This choice is a matter of emotions, that is, it is a matter of desire - what do we indeed want to conserve?

These reflections seem to fall outside biology, but they do not, because they deal with the essence of phylogenic drift - namely they deal with the constitution of lineages through the systemic reproduction of a manner of living basically defined by the preferences that the living systems have at every instant in the course of their living.

Chapter 4
Our Present

We have already said in many ways that biological evolution follows the path of the conservation of any manner of living that constitutes a lineage through its systemic reproductive conservation. And we have also said that evolutionary diversification takes place when variations in the manners of living begin to be conserved through reproduction, and that in this manner new lineages arise either as a branching of the previous ones, or as replacements of old ones that become extinct. Moreover, we have also insisted that in this process the manner of living conserved in a lineage is conserved systemically, through what we call systemic reproduction, and that as a result the genome of the members of the lineage becomes free to change within the constraints defined by the manner of living thus conserved. As a consequence, the systemic conservation of a manner of living may result in a path of genetic drift that facilitates, or makes inevitable, the epigenetic realization of the manner of living conserved through of the members of the lineage in a medium that is arising with them in their epigenesis. In saying this, we are saying that the systemic conservation of behavioral habits channels the path of genetic transformations that take place in the history of a lineage. And we say that this happens when the habits learned by the new members of a lineage as they live alone, with their parents, or with other members of their community, become features of the manner of living conserved.

In these circumstances, one cannot but realize that what will happen in the evolution of our lineage will depend on the manner of living systemically conserved from one generation to another in the living of our children. Will our human identity be conserved as *Homo sapiens-amans*, or will it disappear and something else arise in its place? To answer this question we must reflect on what constitutes our systemic identity as human beings.

Mother / Child Relation

A human being is a manner of living in conversations that arises in each individual human being in the dynamic relation of his or her *Homo sapiens sapiens* bodyhood and the medium formed by other human beings and the rest of the biosphere. That is, the human being occurs in the systemic dynamic interplay of the human manner of living and the *Homo sapiens sapiens* bodyhood. As we have said, this bodyhood has arisen as a result of the particular evolutionary history of conservation of the body transformations that took place along the conservation of languaging as the manner of living that constituted us as human beings.

In the preceding chapters, we have described how we claim that humanness, our humanness as languaging beings with a *Homo sapiens-amans* bodyhood, arose through the conservation of our manner of living as loving neotenic bipedal primates generation after generation in the learning of the children. Therefore, living as *Homo sapiens-amans* makes possible the conservation of the *Homo sapiens-amans* bodyhood, which in turn makes possible living as *Homo sapiens-amans*. Accordingly our identity as *Homo sapiens-amans* is systemic, and will be conserved in the biological and cultural flow our successive generations only as long as the structural and relational dynamics that constitute it as a particular bodyhood and as a particular manner of living, involving both bodyhood and medium, are systemically conserved.

Thus, biologically we are loving beings with a *Homo sapiens-amans* bodyhood that is conserved by our living as *Homo sapiens-amans*, that is as loving human beings. In the following text we shall use the expression "loving humanness" to refer to the *Homo sapiens-amans* manner of being.

The main aspects of living in loving humanness, in the systemic dynamics that makes and conserves that manner of living through our living, are love and play in the intimacy of the mother/child relation. A childhood lived in this manner entails the conservation of self and social respect into adulthood as the basic emotioning that makes possible living in a domain of cooperation, mutual care, play, joy, and beauty. As one of us has shown, the primary mother/child relation is a relation of total trust in body nearness and mutual body acceptance. In this dynamic relation of play with the mother, a child learns his or her body and the body of the other (see Verden-Zöller in Maturana and Verden-Zöller, 1993). Through this process the child develops self and social awareness in self-respect and respect for the other, in self-acceptance and acceptance of the other. At the same time through this process he or she creates the world that he or she lives, and will live, as an expansion of his or her body through his or her relational dynamics. When this primary mother/child relation is not basically disturbed, the condition of loving humanness is directly conserved as a manner of living into adult life. If the mother/child relation is disturbed, but there is at least one other human being with whom the growing child finds total acceptance, trust, and care, the condition of loving humanness can be conserved or recovered through the biology of love.

Let us put this somewhat differently. A human child becomes a singular being as he or she lives his or her relations with other beings, and he or she becomes a loving human being as he or she lives his or her mother/child relation in love and play as a growing child among loving human beings. The fundamental relational dynamics of total body trust in mutual acceptance among human beings, makes and conserves a child as a loving, intelligent, self-respecting, and socially responsible languaging being in a human social domain.

As a child grows in self-respect and respect for others as he or she becomes an individual human being, his or her individuality does not exist or arise in opposition to the social community to which he or she belongs. On the contrary, the child becomes an individual human being as he or she becomes a social being and becomes a social being as he or she becomes an individual human being. If as a child grows, he or she develops a different manner of being than that that is proper to the community to which he or she belongs, he or she will grow as a different being than the other members of the community. Such happening constitutes an opening for a variation in the history of humanness that may lead to another kind of being, culturally or biologically. Whether that happens or not will, of course, depend on whether the new personal identity is conserved as a new manner of living or not in the learning of the children that grow with this person. If the adults also create the conditions under which the new personal identity can indeed be systemically conserved in a new generation, a cultural change takes place. That is, a cultural change happens when a new personal identity begins to be systemically conserved as a new manner of living in a new network of conversations that expands suddenly or progressively into a larger community.

Such a cultural change will be a cultural change only as long as the basic human mother/child relation is conserved. If the basic human pattern of mother/child relation and child upbringing in the generation and conservation of self- and social respect were lost through some change in our cultural manner of living, and if such a change were to be systemically conserved in the generations to come, our human history would undergo more than a cultural change. A new kind of being would appear. Is this now likely to happen?

Patriarchy

Most human beings today live in a patriarchal culture of one kind or another. A patriarchal culture consists in a manner of living centered in appropriation, domination and submission, mistrust and control, sexual and racial discrimination, and war. In a patriarchal culture human coexistence may have many different forms, but it is essentially political. In it relations are viewed mostly as instrumental for gaining superiority in a continuous power struggle, and are lived mostly as such. This political manner of living, however, is not a primary feature of our evolutionary constitution as human beings, which has been, as we have said, an evolutionary history centered on love and mutual trust, not on aggression and mistrust. Our political living is a feature of our currently predominant patriarchal culture that has basically become, as a network of conversations conserved in the learning of our children, a manner of living similar to the manner of living of chimpanzees in a permanent struggle for domination and submission.

That this should be so is not totally unexpected, because cultures arise, like species, in the conservation of some basic manner of living, defined and realized in us human beings as a closed recursive network of conversation around which all else is open to change. Furthermore, what is peculiar to cultures as manners of living in closed networks of conversations is that in the particular dynamic braiding of languaging and emotioning that each one is, it is the particular configuration of emotioning conserved in each that defines its particular character or identity. In these circumstances, a culture that is centered in the emotioning of appropriation and mistrust in the dynamics of domination and submission, is bound to become, sooner or later, a network of conversations of manipulation and control (in a manner of emotioning such as that lived by chimpanzees), and hence, a political culture in a political manner of living. We claim that this is what has happened over the last 7,000 years with the origin of our Western patriarchal culture, as it arose through a change in the living of our ancestors from the emotioning of love and trust to a living in the emotioning of mistrust, appropriation, and control. And this is so much so, that in our daily involvement with our living in patriarchality we have even come to develop theories to justify our political living, pretending that we do so in agreement with our biological conditions to justify our demand on others to comply with the manner of living that we want them to live. Moreover, we are so immersed in the emotioning of mistrust, control, and appropriation that we use our great consensual capacity (namely, our intelligence) to transform those particular aspects of our community living that are the networks of conversations that constitute relational domains such as science, religions, philosophical theories, or money into instrument for political use.

Let us expand here what we have just said about patriarchality, although we have published some of this already in another book (see Maturana and Verden-Zöller, 1993). We, the authors of this essay, claim that political living began to be a manner of living in us humans as patriarchy began as a culture with the conservation of a manner of living in appropriation, enmity, mistrust, control, valuing of procreation, and war. We think that this happened as a cultural change through the constitution of pastoral life in Asia among the people who later became the Indo-Europeans who invaded a matristic Europe. A cultural change occurs when the closed network of conversations that defines and conserves a culture changes. We think that for a cultural change to occur, the configuration of emotioning that guides the flow of the network of conversations of the original culture must change, and the new emotioning thus arising must be conserved through the new manner of living that it brings about. And we claim that patriarchy appeared in that way, when the configuration of emotioning of the non-patriarchal culture from which it arose changed into the particular new one that constitutes patriarchality in a dynamics that contributed to its conservation. We propose in what follows, in a synthetic manner, an imagined scenario of how such a change might have taken place in a spontaneous not-intended dynamics:

In one of the families that lived by following some herds of migratory animals, accompanied at some distance by wolves that fed on the same herd as they, the adults begun to interfere with the free access of the wolves to the animals of the herd that were their natural food. As those adults did so, they must have done it in the conscious or unconscious awareness that the exclusion of the wolf from his natural food was a circumstantial violation of the natural coherences of life in which all animals and plants have a proper, legitimate place. Most likely the adults made some ritual that conserved their awareness of the violation of the natural order with what they were doing; perhaps those adults even apologized to the wolves for interfering with their free access to the herd. The motives that the adults had in excluding the wolves from their natural food could have been any. But if on some occasion, for whatever circumstance, they did not explain to their children that what they were doing was a violation of the natural order of existence, some of their children may have grown up without being aware of the sacred relation of partnership that existed between the humans and the wolves as well as between the wolves and the animals on which they fed. As that happened, those children grew treating the exclusion of the wolves from their natural food as something proper to the legitimate order of existence. In this process, the configuration of emotioning lived by those children changed with respect to that of their parents, and the emotion of appropriation appeared in their living as a matter of course, giving legitimacy to their behavior as they began to restrict the mobility of the herds to "protect the animals from the aggression of the wolves."

But appropriation brings with it the loss of trust in the formerly accepted natural coherences of the world, and the protection of the herds sooner or later resulted in the persecution of the wolf, who was eventually exterminated in order to gain security against him. With that, the emotions that constitute enmity and aggression appeared as legitimate emotional fundaments for the actions of appropriation and control as a manner of living, and the instruments of hunting, which were originally used with awe and gratitude for the food that they brought, became weapons when they began to be systematically used to exterminate the wolf in the emotions of enmity, aggression, and arrogance. Furthermore, under the circumstances of mistrust, and in the fear that the enmity with the wolf carried (as it was always coming back for its legitimate food), actions of control appeared in the desire for security. Thus, the procreation of the animals of the herd and of the members of the family become a matter of active concern as a manner of living in the design of a relational space that would assure survival. In this manner the whole former configuration of emotioning (trust, participation, respect for all living beings, sharing, mutual acceptance, veneration for the sacredness of existence) that defined and conserved the original non-patriarchal conversations of the family changed, and a different one appeared that constituted a new manner of living centered in appropriation, mistrust, control, arrogance, valuing of procreation, enmity, aggression, and war. Finally, as trust in the natural coherences of existence was lost, living in the search of security led to the emotioning that permitted manipulation of others, cheating and political relations as a natural manner of living learned as a feature of their natural growth by the children. That is, the pastoral patriarchal culture begun.

As pastoral patriarchal living became established, the herds grew under the protection (that is, control) of the pastoral families, the growth of the families themselves through the valuing of procreation and rejection of any notion of birth control, overpopulation, overgrazing, ecological distortions, poverty or the menace of poverty, and eventually migration, all appeared as spontaneous results. The migrations also led to the meeting with other human communities that were treated in the same way as the wolf, that is, destroyed or appropriated, if there was not emotional coincidence with them. In this process the whole network of patriarchal conversations must have arisen with all its features, from hierarchical discriminations, through slavery and the violent appropriation of the sex of foreign women by the patriarchal men for domination, submission, and political use. As all this happened, the establishment of the emotioning of the pastoral patriarchal culture entailed such a complete change with respect to the emotioning of the matristic culture from which it arose, that when in the course of their migrations the pastoral patriarchal people encountered the matristic communities of Europe, they saw everything in them as fully inimical to their own existence.

In such circumstances the only possible result of that encounter for the pastoral patriarchal people was war with the aim of the total negation and destruction of such a contradictory manner of living. But not all the matristic communities were fully destroyed; some were displaced and in others the men were killed and the women were appropriated by the patriarchal men to be enslaved and for sexual use and abuse.

Cultures, as networks of conversations, are composed by human beings of both sexes. The expression *patriarchal* is not to be associated with men only; similarly the expression *matristic* is not to be associated only with women. In a patriarchal culture both women and men are patriarchal, and in a matristic culture both men and women are matristic. Matristic and patriarchal cultures are different manners of living, different forms of relating, different manners of emotioning; that is, different closed networks of conversations that are realized in each case by both men and women. Therefore, there is no basic contradiction between men and women in a pastoral patriarchal or in a matristic culture, because in both cultures men and women grow homogeneously patriarchal or matristic. A basic contradiction arises between adult men and women when boys and girls are brought up to become members of different cultures at different moments of their upbringing, which is what we think happens in our Western patriarchal culture. Let us expand this notion.

We think that the pastoral patriarchal culture began in its origin as an homogeneous culture in which men and women became naturally patriarchal, and without contradictions between them as they grew both equally immersed in the patriarchal conversations. The same must have happened with the women and men in the matristic culture. But when the pastoral patriarchal people encountered the matristic ones, and by warfare the patriarchal men appropriated the matristic women after killing or enslaving the matristic men, in many matristic communities the women did not fully submit, and complied with the patriarchal demands only to the extent that such compliance allowed them to protect their children. We think that we members of our Western patriarchal culture come from such a situation, and that our Western patriarchal culture is the result of a cultural hybridization in which the matristic women managed to some extent to conserve their matristic culture in their relation with other women and with their children, constituting a matristic family core in the midst of an adult male patriarchal living. We still live this hybrid existence in our Western culture as we grow as children in a matristic milieu and then at puberty enter a patriarchal adulthood. As a result, children of both sexes in our Western patriarchal culture live what is a cultural opposition between their matristic mother and their patriarchal father as if such opposition were an intrinsic contradiction between man and woman. At the same time, in our Western patriarchal culture, children of both sexes live a conflictive cultural transition from a matristic childhood to a patriarchal adulthood as if this were a psychological transition proper to their natural psychological development.

Political existence destroys intimacy, as it is founded on relations of domination and submission, not on relations of love. Whatever trust there is in it, or appears to be in it, is transitory, either because it is hypocritical, or because it is instrumental in a political design. Thus, in a political coexistence sex stops being the foundation for intimacy and the most basic source of pleasure in human relations, and becomes an instrument for political manipulation. Political life endangers the conservation of the mother/child relation as a relation of total trust and mutual body acceptance in play, and interferes with the proper child upbringing in the emotioning of self- and social respect that constitutes the fundament of our human identity. Moreover, this happens because as political life instrumentalizes all relations, it also instrumentalizes child upbringing by making it a function of designs for the future. This focusing on preparation for a role in a political life separates the child and the mother from the present of their living in mutual acceptance and mutual trust (see Maturana and Verden-Zöller, 1993). As a result, in our historical present the expansion of the patriarchal emotioning, that leads to the utilization of all human relations as political as well as commercial instruments, makes it almost impossible for a child to grow spontaneously in a manner centered in the biology of love. In this process, self- and social respect, cooperation and mutual trust, and the expansion of intelligence that the biology of love entails, become features of life that require to be reflected upon in order to be realized as desired aspects of the conservation of humanness. That is, we must now create a rational justification for having love as features of the child's upbringing through the expansion of our understanding if we wish to conserve loving humanness, because love is fading away from the spontaneous world of the child.

Political Existence

Patriarchality, through its emotioning centered on appropriation, mistrust, control, discrimination, and aggression, has transformed the basically cooperative trusting human living into a competitive, struggling, and cheating political coexistence. We modern patriarchal human beings live immersed in our political living, and we do not realize that political coexistence restricts the development of a person as a fully self-respecting individual who can decide for him or herself how to act responsibly in the community to which he or she belongs. A self-respecting person does not depend on the opinion of others, or on the image that he or she projects, or on the appearance of his or her behavior to others, to act adequately according to the well-being of the community to which he or she belongs, because to the extent that he or she lives in self-respect and respect for the other, he or she acts spontaneously in a fully socially responsible manner. The present expansion of patriarchy into early childhood through the demand on the mothers to prepare their children, boys and girls, for their respective roles in a life of competition and appearances, makes the growing boys and girls incapable of being fully responsible for their lives and for the worlds that they bring about in their living. This is because the patriarchal identities that they are demanded to fulfill are based on appropriation, control, manipulations, competition, mistrust, and the continuous lies entailed in valuing appearances, salesmanship, and deceit instead of self-respect, sincerity, and honesty. Courage, audacity, and bravery lose their value as expressions of social responsibility and self-respect proper to living in the biology of love, and become instead aggressiveness and arrogance, war-like virtues and political arguments for interpersonal manipulations proper to living in a patriarchal culture.

Finally, political coexistence negates sensuality and tenderness as all relations become manipulative, and restricts intelligence, cooperation, and participation because it focuses the attention of daily living mostly on one fundamental theme—namely, domination and submission. But modern humanity does not live exclusively in political strife, or "monkey business," as we occasionally call it. There is also an attempt to live in democracy, in a neomatristic coexistence as an endeavor of cooperation in the common project of living in mutual respect in the biology of love. Democracy arose as a manner of living that breaks with patriarchality, and as such the intent in its declaration as a desirable manner of coexistence was to create an extended community life founded on relations of self-and mutual respect as the grounding for the common enterprise that is the creation of an honest social life (see Maturana in Maturana and Verden-Zöller, 1993). Yet, for this intended manner of living to happen, the matristic human child upbringing must be conserved. But, how?

Human Upbringing

The identity of a system as a particular case of a given kind has two dimensions. One dimension is the organization that defines its class identity, the other is its manner of relating and interacting in the medium in which it exists. Accordingly, a particular system conserves its individual identity only as long as it conserves its organization and its manner of relating and interacting through the structural changes that it undergoes as a result of its own internal dynamics modulated by the structural changes triggered in it by its interactions. It follows, then, that in these circumstances the identity of any system lasts as long as its interactions in the medium constitute a systemic dynamics in which its structural changes, the structural changes of the medium, and the flow of the recursive interactions between the system and the medium result in the conservation of the organization and manner of relating that constitutes and defines the identity of the system. In the case of living systems, one of the basic consequences of this situation is that their structures and the structure of the medium in which they exist change congruently while their different identities are systemically conserved, both along their evolution (through reproduction) and along their particular individual histories. The identity of any living system as a living system of a particular kind, is not an intrinsic feature of the bodyhood that realizes it, nor is it an intrinsic feature of the manner of living of the living system that lives it, but it arises as a configuration of relations conserved through the recursive interplay of the manner of living and the bodyhood of the living system in the flow of the structural changes that it undergoes in its interactions in the medium.

In such a recursive dynamics, the continuous structural changes of the living system follow a course that arises moment after moment in the realization and conservation of its manner of living. As a result, a living system conserves its particular identity as long as the configuration of relations that constitutes it is conserved through the flow of its interaction in the medium while it lives. So the identity of a living system entails at any moment both its structure and its manner of living in a recursive interplay of both, and none gives rise to it separated from the other.

This results in two things that once said appear obvious: one, that we human beings have the bodyhood that we have as a result of an evolutionary history of conservation of the loving human being manner of living in conversations; and two, that existing in conversations does not by itself constitute humanness, the *Homo sapiens-amans* bodyhood is also necessary. In us loving human beings, therefore, the continuous recursive braiding of our bodyhood dynamics and our *Homo sapiens-amans* manner of living results in the systemic dynamics that conserves our:

(a) condition of being *Homo sapiens-amans* as long as we live as loving human beings;

(b) *Homo sapiens-amans* bodyhood as a bodyhood proper to the realization of the *Homo sapiens-amans* manner of living as long as we live as loving human beings; and

(c) existence as a space open to unending recursive changes in the world that we bring forth in our living as we live as languaging beings living as *Homo sapiens-amans*.

To be a loving human it is not enough to be born with a *Homo sapiens-amans* anatomy and physiology, it is also necessary to live in a loving manner in a community of loving human beings. Living as a *Homo sapiens-amans* among *Homo sapiens-amans* constitutes the systemic dynamics in which living as a loving human being is realized and conserved.

As we conserve that which makes us human beings, we open a space for unending changes in the worlds that we bring forth as languaging beings without losing the human identity. Moreover, human beingness is a manner of living in interpersonal relations, not a form or manner of handling an independent world. Thus, human beingness can be realized through many different ways of handling objects and things in many different closed networks of conversations that are lived as different cultures. That is, as long as the human being manner of living in conversations is conserved in the succession of generations of *Homo sapiens*, all the structural changes in the human bodyhood will be changes in the conservation of the *Homo sapiens* bodyhood, and all the changes in its manner of relating will take place as cultural changes around the conservation of the human beingness in the realization of generations of human beings.

Therefore the upbringing of the children as human beings is and has been central in the course of human history as a history of constitution and conservation of the human beingness. The history of human beingness is carried by children, not by adults—even though adults make the present through their living. Children learn to be whatever they become by living with others, and they become adults of one kind or another according to how the adults with which they live, live. It is for these reasons that we claim that the upbringing of a child takes place as a transformation in coexistence, and that human loving humanness will be conserved or lost through the upbringing of the children.

If our children grow in a mother/child relation of total mutual trust and body acceptance through play when they are babies and in their early childhood (see Verden-Zöller in Maturana and Verden-Zöller, 1993), loving humanness will be conserved through them. As they grow in this way, they will become adults in an ambiance that fosters self- and social respect. In such trust and acceptance, the child is never corrected in his or her being, only in his or her doings. Whenever we correct the being of a child (not merely as an occasional happening but as a manner of living with him or her) by telling how he or she should or should not be, we deny him or her, we tell him or her that he or she is somehow wrongly made, and destroy his or her self-respect and self-acceptance. As we do that, we close the human world to the child. If instead we correct the doings of a child by inviting him or her to reflect on the procedures that have to be employed for producing a particular desired result, allowing him or her the freedom to act from his or her self-awareness, we do not deny the child, as we do not correct his or her being. As we invite the child to observe and act from the perspective of his or her own awareness and choice, we confirm him or her in self-acceptance and self-respect, and open a space for his or her autonomous doings in self- and social respect. In so doing, we open the human world for the child, incorporating him or her within it (see also Appendix 8).

If the mother/child relation is interfered with, and the child does not grow living in self-respect and self-acceptance, he or she will become a kind of being that is restricted or limited in his or her capacity of living the biology of love. If such a thing were to happen, the capacity of the child to live in the intimacy basic for a healthy family relation would be impaired. Fortunately, we modern human beings still consider such a manner of child development inadequate, and we still consider that the adult who grows from such a childhood becomes an unhealthy adult in need of a therapy that recovers love. And that therapy still works.

Psychic Existence

We human beings have a *Homo sapiens* bodyhood, but our human existence is relational. Human existence, that is, human beingness, is a manner of relating, and as such it is multidimensional. However, not all the dimensions of the relational existence of a human being are at any instant equally accessible to his or her reflexive awareness, or to the distinction of an observer. Many, perhaps most, of the dimensions of our relational existence as human beings are beyond our awareness, and are, therefore, unconscious. Furthermore, the whole relational domain in which a living being exists arises in the relations that it lives through the interplay of its dynamic structure and the dynamic structure of the medium in which it happens to live. Through such interplay the living being contributes to the systemic dynamics that creates the medium in which it exists, in a process that happens simply through its living. We call the relational domain in which a living being exists its *relational psychic space*.

To the extent that we exist in language, we human beings differ from other living beings in that we live at any instant in a relational psychic space that has conscious and unconscious dimensions according to whether these are or are not accessible to our reflexive awareness at that instant. Furthermore, each of us lives as the same all the situations that occur to us as equal configurations of conscious and/or unconscious relations in our psychic space. Indeed, whenever we live something that we experience as the "same," we treat it as the same. So we call the same two situations that we cannot distinguish in our experience, regardless of how different they may appear to an external or independent observer. This operational condition of our existence as living beings is the basis for what we call illusions, mistakes, or virtual realities—as experiences that we live as valid in our emotioning while they happen to us, but which we later invalidate in our reflections through reference to, or in comparison with some other experiences that we consider at that instant of more basic validity. In other words, it is a constitutive condition of the living of all living beings that nothing that happens to them or in them in their relational existence is irrelevant for the course of their living, regardless of whether an observer may claim that what the living being is living is an illusion. This means that for us human beings nothing that we live in the flow of our emotioning, whether consciously or unconsciously, is irrelevant or "virtual" in our living. There are no virtual emotions (in general, nothing is virtual in our psychic existence), and the course of our doings is always modulated by our emotioning, regardless of whether we are conscious or not of what we live, and this is so even when we claim that we are aware that what we are living is a mere illusion.

Furthermore, and more specifically, all the emotions that we live as human beings, regardless of whether we are conscious of them or not, and regardless of whether they arise in us through unconscious or conscious relations, are relevant to our reasoning because our emotions guide the course of our reasoning by specifying the conscious and unconscious fundaments on which our reasoning stands at any moment. At the same time, in the recursive dynamics of the operation of our nervous system, the flow of our reasoning modulates our emotioning. Further, as our emotions change, they modulate the course of our reasoning so that it too may change. In different words: our conscious and unconscious psychic existence modulates our emotioning as well as our reasoning through specifying the emotional grounding on which our reasoning stands, and our conscious and unconscious reasoning modulates the flow of our emotioning. That this should be so is a spontaneous outcome of our relational existence in the interplay of our bodyhood and our manner of living, so that as our bodyhood changes, the flow of our living changes, and as the flow of our living changes, our bodyhood changes too (see Appendix 3). Indeed, our different individual identities as different particular manners of human beingness that exist as relational entities, are psychic identities; that is, they take place in a psychic relational space that we consciously and unconsciously continuously create with our living. Even more, our psychic identity, our conscious and unconscious manner of relating in the psychic space, is systemic and is systemically conserved in our living as our living participates both in the modulation of our bodyhoods and in the arising of the medium in which we live.

Let us now look more deeply into this matter. Our emotioning, as a flow in our manner of relating in the world we live, can be conscious or unconscious according to whether we are aware or not of the relational dimensions of our psychic space. We can comment, reason, argue, or reflect on what we do or distinguish in our relational dynamics. We can claim that we live an illusion, or that we committed a mistake and that we are aware now that what we did before was not right; or we can claim that we lived or are living a virtual reality and not what actually is in our realization as living systems. But in all cases, and no matter how we reason or how convinced we are of our arguments, the conscious and unconscious emotioning that we live is never trivial and cannot be undone, because what happens in our psychic existence is never virtual as it modulates the course of our living.

We cannot distinguish in our experience between perception and illusion. An illusion is an experience that we devaluate in relation to another experience that we consider valid as a perception; a perception is an experience that we validate through another experience that we consider undoubtedly valid or more obviously valid as a perception than the first one. That is, illusions and perceptions are afterthoughts, reflective judgments about the validity of our experiences. We live all experiences as equally valid in the moment that we live them, even if they are not all equally acceptable or desirable to us as we reflect rationally about them, or as we reflect about the nature of the human relations that these experiences entail. So, virtual realities are virtual only in the domain of reflections, and we flow in our living according to how we reflect on the realities we live.

Our reflections and our reasonings are not trivial to our living as human beings either; they modulate the course of our emotioning, and in that sense they are fundamental to the course of our living. Through reasoning and reflection we can braid our rational with our emotional awareness, and thus we can be responsible for both our emotioning and our reasoning as we contemplate these from the perspective of our desires. In these circumstances, then, it is not perception, or illusion, or reality that matters as we attempt to guide the flow of our living as human beings, but it is what we desire as our domain of psychic existence for ourselves and for our children. What matters is the psychic identity that we consciously or unconsciously conserve in our daily living (see also Appendix 8).

Psychic Identity

By the very fact that we human beings exist in conversations, our individual existence as human beings takes place in a recursive network of conscious and unconscious interactions that arises through our living in a systemically conserved domain of psychic coexistence. In these circumstances, it is our living in a multidimensional psychic space of conscious and unconscious interactions that guides and has guided the transformation of our bodyhoods in structural coupling within our different domains of existence as we realize our human beingness by living in that very same psychic space. And it is through those transformations of our bodyhoods that we systemically conserve those particular psychic identities that we learn to live by living them through conscious and unconscious relations in a human domain, as we grow from babyhood. And what do we learn as we learn? We learn to relate, to see, to hear, to smell, to touch, to prefer, to dislike, to think . . . that is, we learn a manner of relating, a manner of emotioning, and we acquire a psychic identity as the particular configuration of emotioning that defines us, and which we conserve by living in it.

The kind of being, or the kind of human being we become along our lives, is, therefore, determined by the conscious and unconscious psychic coexistence that we live as we grow, realizing a particular psychic identity in a particular human community. This psychic identity is systemically conserved through our body dynamics as we operate in the human community in which we arise as human beings, but it is also modulated by what we live in the other domains of interactions in which we also exist. We change our doings, we change what we manipulate, and we change the form of the rational arguments that we develop to justify or to deny our emotioning as we grow and become adults, but we conserve systemically the psychic identity that we learned to live and to generate as little children through living it. We do this unaware of what we do through systemically conserving the configuration of emotioning that defines our psychic identity as we co-create with other beings the human community in which that particular psychic identity takes place as the natural manner of being. That is, we conserve a manner of seeing, a manner of reacting, a manner of reflecting, a manner of valuing . . . as we conserve the psychic identity that we live through living as members of the community in which such psychic identity is our natural manner of being. We may generate theories and ideologies that support or deny that psychic identity, but no matter how we reason, we conserve our psychic identity by living the configuration of emotioning that constitutes it and in which our reasoning takes place, unless we change our psychic identity. Moreover, the theories about ourselves and our world that we generate may become, and frequently do become part of the constitution of our living or of the circumstances in which our psychic identity is conserved until we change. But, given all this, how can a psychic identity change?

We learn to live the particular psychic existence that arises through the configuration of emotioning that we live as babies and children. It is the emotioning entailed in what we hear, see, touch, smell, or say, or in what is said to us, that constitutes our psychic existence. It is the emotioning entailed in the relations and encounters as we live consciously and unconsciously with others, or with ourselves in our reflections as we grow, that defines our psychic existence. But it is particularly those aspects of our lives that we live unconsciously, because we cannot reflect about the emotions involved in them, that will define most of our psychic existence as we acquire the psychic identity that we will systemically conserve in our living. We cannot at any moment live a psychic identity different from the one that we have learned and conserve systemically in the flow of our living. This is so precisely because learning consists in the congruent structural transformations of the body and the medium along the life of an animal that a person can only generate in his or her structural dynamics, the relations proper to the psychic identity that he or she has learned to live and conserve systemically in his or her living as he or she generates at the same time the medium in which that psychic identity takes place and is conserved. Are we trapped?

If our parents are aggressive with each other or with us, we develop an aggressive unconscious psychic dynamics as we grow, even if we do not like it. If as small children we see aggression in television as if it were the natural manner of living, and even if we know that what happens there is only virtual reality, we develop an unconscious psychic aggressive dynamics, and we have great difficulty avoiding living in aggression. Moreover, as we develop an unconscious aggressive psychic identity, our whole existence becomes permeated by it as we do not know how to operate differently because we live in the systemic relational dynamics that conserves our living in aggression as the natural way of being.

If as children we have been submitted to the aggression and abuse of adults, and the course of life frees us from such abuse without our direct participation, our unconscious psychic relational space does not change with that liberation. We remain aggressive as we continue to live as if aggressive and abusive behavior towards children and others were the natural manner of relating with them. This will indeed remain so unless we intentionally change or chose to be different through an emotional change that arises through our becoming aware of what we do and of what we want to do. And, yes, we can change. Our psychic identity can change, and indeed does change if the manner of our emotioning changes in the course of our living as we enter in conflicting domains of actions through contradictory emotions. Indeed, this occurs when love appears and opens our vision in relation to our contradictory emotioning with respect to others or to ourselves. When that happens, as one accepts in the emotional domain the present that one lives in its legitimacy regardless of whether it is desirable or not, one becomes open to changing that present in an act of self-love and self-respect. In that opening, the whole systemic dynamics of our living as our manner of relating changes, and in that process a new configuration of emotioning emerges that we may begin to conserve in our living as our new psychic identity.

Moreover, such a shift in our psychic identity may occur through aware reflection as an operation in our emotional domain as we operate in self-acceptance and self-respect, and we distinguish our present as something that we can contemplate. Therefore, reflection is basically an operation in our emotioning as we release our certainties and an operation in languaging in the operational dynamics that makes possible our reflexive looking at ourselves. As we do that we can see our manner of relating, violent or serene, friendly or aggressive, hard or tender, indifferent or caring, and we can see whether we like or do not like the psychic identity that we see and act accordingly. Without self-love, self-acceptance, or self-respect there is no reflection, precisely because reflection entails releasing one's certainties in an operation that opens a relational space to look within one's own emotional dynamics as a source for actions. But at the same time, without the operationality of living as a languaging being, there is no way in which one could reflect and distinguish oneself as an independent entity.

Therefore, our manner of relating and living with others, that is our psychic identity, can change through an act of intended assertion of our dignity as a result of our reflective awareness of our emotioning in self-respect and self-acceptance. Reason may help us to shift our psychic identify if it guides our emotioning, but does not do so by itself. It is not a matter of behaving or not behaving according to reason, because what changes when there is a shift in the psychic relational space that one lives is the emotioning, not the coherence of a rational argument. At any moment we live in the only way that we know, and we do not even have the possibility of being aware of this unless we release our hold on our certainties and we reflect as an act in our emotioning. We repeat: only reflection can liberate us as an act that will appear to us and others as a choice, but a reflection is an act that begins with an emotional shift and is not an operation of pure reason. The emotional change that usually opens a space for such a shift is love, that is the acceptance of the legitimacy of oneself, of the others, and of the circumstances that one does not like and wants to change. Without love there is not emotional opening to act in responsibility and freedom.

Sex and Spirituality

As languaging beings we human beings have lived and live a history of changing domains of existence. Indeed, as recursions take place in our living in consensual coordinations of consensual coordinations of behaviors, new domains of objects and relations between objects arise in our conversations that become the ground for our living in new experiential domains that can become our permanent basic existential abode. These new domains of existence arise in us languaging beings in two basic ways;

namely, through the distinction of new kinds of experiences and through the adoption of new manners of explaining experiences. Furthermore, as these new domains of existence arise, they arise intercrossing with the previous domains of existence in which the human beings lived. As this happens, the new domains arise historically embedded in the previous ones and become openings for new modes of existence that may become new manners of living in the systemic conservation of the new biological and psychic identities that appear as we live these new modes of existence.

We think that individualized expanded sexual intimacy is one of the relational dimensions that has given rise to a new domain of existence in the evolutionary history that gave origin to us human beings. As sexuality and sexual intercourse began to be lived in the pleasure and trust of individualized intimacy, it brought about permanence in the couple and family as well as an expansion of the awareness of the body unity with a particular other and with the realm of his or her existence. And we also think that this expansion of the awareness of body unity with a particular other and his or her realm of existence also gave rise to the awareness of the domain of spiritual experiences as those experiences of expansion of conscious awareness of the unity of all.

All human beings now and then have spontaneous experiences of expansion of their awareness of participation and inclusion in some wider realm of relations than the particular one of their restricted individuality, in a conscious vision of belonging in it as a basic feature of their existence. Such an experience is usually referred to or described with awe and is what is indicated when speaking of a spiritual experience. In a spiritual experience the other and the others (the earth, the cosmos, the community, nature, the biosphere, the living, the goddess or gods, depending on the culture to which one belongs) acquire an intimate, close presence. Not only do the other or others become recognizable participants in one's existence, but also one becomes a participant in theirs, and one is aware of it.

But, how is this experience possible? We think that whenever some particular relational experience with another becomes individualized and has recurrent presence in the domain of love, the experience of expansion of awareness of unity with a wider relational realm, as well as of participation in its existence, becomes possible as one begins to be attentive, as well as consciously and unconsciously concerned with the circumstances of the existence of the other. Moreover, we think that once a spiritual experience has been lived, the psychic joy as well as the physiological well-being lived in it brings the desire to live it again, or to expand it as a manner of daily living in some basic domain proper to the culture to which one belongs.

We think that the deep psychic and physiological well-being of the mother/child relation of total body acceptance in mutual trust, is the fundament for the spiritual experience in early childhood, and that the well being of friendship is an opening for its occurrence later in life. But more deeply, and in a more total and overwhelmingly basic manner yet, we think that *sexual intimacy with a particular other, as it has arisen in the course of our neotenic history as an expansion of the acceptance in trust and pleasure of the nearness of the body of another, is the basic and most fundamental occasion for spiritual experiences in our lineage.* The intensity of an orgasm lived in the joy of the tender and sensual nearness of a particular other makes everything related to him or her a source of care that increases the desire of being together with him or her in the acceptance of all. When sexuality takes place in the acceptance and enjoyment of the nearness of another in the fullness of the behavioral acceptance of his or her total legitimacy, that is when sexuality takes place in the biology of love, then orgasm is a particular ecstatic moment within the breadth of the loving relationship.

Lived in this way, sexuality carries with it serenity and the joy of full nearness in mutual contemplation. At the same time, through the opening of intelligence and the expansion of awareness that love brings, there is also an expansion of the awareness and understanding of the circumstances in which one is with the other. Indeed, love is the only emotion that opens intelligence and expands awareness. One sees more, hears more, touches more, smells more, understands more when in the biology of love. And love does so precisely because it occurs as a relational domain in the behaviors through which the others, or better, all others, arise as legitimate others in coexistence with oneself.

Whenever there is a sense of well-being in just being in the easy acceptance of the circumstances in which one is, there is a possibility for that which we acknowledge as spirituality in our daily life. When we become aware of this wellbeing, we encounter it as a spiritual experience, even today. Yes, spirituality is an easy natural experience of belonging in everything as a spontaneous manner of relating in the unity of all. Such a natural manner of living in the connectedness of existence can frequently be observed in animals in the wild, especially in mammals, when they sit in quiet contemplation of their surroundings, particularly in the evening, when the dimming of the lights and sounds of the day makes all things sharp and still. Non-languaging animals are not reflectively aware of their connectedness the way we are, they just live it.

Our awareness of the interconnected unity of all existence in the biosphere (or the cosmos) is a result of the features of our biology as languaging animals. Accordingly, it is through reflection that human sexuality in all its dimensions — but particularly in the tenderness, joy, intimacy, and quietness of a chosen individualized embrace and copulation — that the awareness of the other and of his or her realm of connectedness has the possibility of becoming a cosmic presence. Human orgasm as a more or less prolonged and deep experience in the awareness of unity with the other in the oblivion of being in full togetherness, takes place in the trust of total acceptance. Through that trust and total acceptance, sexuality expands tenderness and sensuality in the completeness of a full unity with the whole existence. And in that sexuality, orgasm, when lived in the sensuality and tenderness of an expanding neoteny, we think, may have constituted the primary source of full awareness of the spiritual experience in our lineage of languaging animals. In a tender, sensual, and individualized sexual relation, the spiritual experience just happens — no intent is needed. Yet, for the reflective awareness of that experience it is necessary to live in language, and when that reflection happens, the connectedness of that experience with all existence becomes overwhelming.

We claim that we humans beings owe our possibility of an aware spiritual existence to the expansion of the sexuality of the females in our neotenic lineage. Moreover, we assert that it was the expansion of the sexuality of the females of our ancestors that made possible and conserved in their living together the closeness and intimacy that created the relational space in which languaging could arise and be conserved in the learning of the children as the manner of living that defined and constituted our human lineage. Furthermore, this basic connection between sexuality and the spiritual experience is apparent in that the experience of unity with the cosmos, with a goddess, with God, or with nature is frequently evoked or described by mystics as an orgasmic experience of love. At the same time, the spiritual experience is so basic in human life that it is not strange that in non-patriarchal cultures, the experience of the sacred and spiritual should be sensed and lived as a feature of daily life in full coherence with the unity of all beings. In those cultures the sacred is lived as living in harmony with the cosmos in its easy and spontaneous dynamics of continuous generation and transformation in cycles of life and death. Nor is it strange, either, that in matristic cultures the sacred and spiritual existence should be evoked with the image of a mother goddess that creates and destroys, in a never-ending present that arises and disappears cyclically in the background of her totality. And, in the same context, it is not strange that in non-patriarchal cultures the mother goddess should be seen as an evocation of the coherent coexistence of all living beings in their spontaneous natural systemic abundance, and not as a fertility power of monotonic linear productivity. Finally, it is not strange that in matristic cultures what we call cultic rituals and spiritual ceremonies should be lived as occasions for the enaction, the recovery, or the expansion of the awareness of human inclusion in the unity of all existence, in a process that allows one to see oneself anew as part of the interconnectedness of everything, in awe and joy for its ever-present beauty

Different religions and philosophies explain the spiritual experience through different theories, and their followers have invented, proposed, and adopted many different practices to obtain and to conserve it as a feature of their daily lives. All those different practices lead to an expansion of the experience of awareness of the practitioners' inclusion and participation in a wider realm of existence. As long as they conserve their expanded awareness by remaining non-religious and non-political in their relational actions. That is, the expanded awareness happens only as long as the persons who live it abandon all attempts to control the flow of their lives as they rely on their total trust in the coherences of existence. That is, all practices oriented to attain a state of effortless daily spiritual existence or enlightenment operate through releasing all ego attachment while conserving full reflexive awareness.

Through the expansion of the female sexuality in a male/female neotenic sexual coexistence in the biology of intimacy, human history began, and it has mostly been a spontaneous spiritual history until the last few thousand years. Spirituality in human history must have been lived as a matter of course in the daily experience of human inclusion in the realm of all existing beings until the distinction of the spiritual experience as a manipulable entity was made. When in the course of history such a distinction was made, spirituality became an object of attention, reflection and intent, and as it thus became an explicit and special manner of being to be specially sought after, it became separate and distant. As the spiritual experience became something to be attained, spirituality became a domain of speaking about something difficult to reach and different from the immediate domains of existence in which human beings could easily live their daily lives. When that happened, human existence changed; it stopped being naturally spiritual as a feature of daily life, and theories as particular manners of explaining human life (experience) with elements of human life (experiences) changed, too. As a consequence, a new human identity appeared in which sexuality stopped being the basic grounding of human spiritual existence, and became both an argument in the constructions of explanations of human life, and, eventually through patriarchality, an instrument for the manipulation of political relations.

As the theories by which explain our life change our domains of existence, our emotioning changes too, and what may have been until then acceptable or even sacred as different aspects of human relations and connectedness with all beings can become undesirable. Through this process, in the spontaneous dynamics of our human living and in the recursive generation of new entities and relations in language, new explanations may arise and have arisen as part of an open-ended flow of cultural conservation and change. And as this happened along our Western patriarchal history, logic began to displace emotions in the core of aware human living, and spirituality became philosophical or religious, losing its full presence in daily life. Human beings stopped seeing themselves as natural components of the living realm and became special. As a result, and in different degrees in the different forms taken by our Western patriarchal culture, sexuality stopped being the fundament of our spiritual experiences, and children began to be taught that sex was for reproduction, in an implicit context that used sex for political manipulation. In this process, sex in the psychic space of our Western culture stopped being lived as basic source of pleasure in the joy of a coexistence in tenderness and mutual care, or as an opening for the enlightening experience of cosmic unity in the nearness of the other in full mutual trust and total body acceptance.

Yes, total body acceptance in mutual trust in a human sexual embrace is a basic experience of cosmic unity in human life, and as such it has in itself nothing to do with reproduction. Moreover, a spiritual experience, as an experience of reflective awareness of the unity of all existing beings, is an experience of acceptance of the body of the other in total trust proper to the mother/child relation that is also lived in our neotenic condition as a feature of our adult life. As sexual intercourse must have been lived by our early ancestors as a source of pleasure and not of procreation, pregnancy and birth must have appeared to them as a spontaneous natural manifestation of life through the female in its continuous changing present, and as nothing special in the easy comfort of an innocent spiritual living. But with the distinction of the spiritual experience as something different from daily life, all changed, and the psychic relational existence of the human beings that made such a distinction shifted as spirituality became a distant condition to be desired and searched for in an attempt to recover its presence.

The human manner of living is not genetically determined but rather is systemically generated and conserved. The genetic constitution and the initial somatic structure are the starting point. *What is determined in the moment of conception of an organism by its genetic constitution and its initial somatic structure, is its structural starting point.* The structural starting point of an organism specifies for it the domain of its possible ontogenies. However, which ontogeny takes place through its life history, and where it takes place, occurs through an epigenetic process in a historical dynamics that results from the interplay of the initial structure of the organism and the circumstances of the medium in which it happens to live. Accordingly, we humans can live along successive generations all the different kinds of lives (that is, cultures, worlds) that we may generate through different theories as we invent them to explain, to justify, or to modulate our emotions, if they are conserved and reproduced systemically in the learning of our children. With the advent of patriarchality a new domain of relations and distinctions arose as a new manner of psychic existence, namely, that of mistrust and control, or politics. And with this new manner of psychic existence, there also arose the theoretical justification of the control and domination of the life of others through notions of hierarchy and authority, of good and evil, of superiority and inferiority, with the corresponding implicit blindness about those others.

In this process sex became degraded by being submitted to patriarchal authority as all relations in that political psychic space have to be, because the spontaneous enlightening presence of sexuality when lived in love could not be controlled, and the freedom of action and reflection that it brought to the relational domain was a menace to the patriarchy. In the process of expansion of patriarchality, spiritual blindness as a feature of ordinary coexistence also expanded. Interpersonal innocence was largely lost through the political use of human relations, and values appeared as special aspects of human relations, separated from the flow of daily life, and hence had to be taught. As values appeared in the context of patriarchality, they acted as instruments for directing or controlling human behavior under the guise of preserving humanness, thus giving rise to a manner of living that spontaneously became basically dishonest.

Yet, in its origin human life must have been fundamentally spiritual, not political, as it arose in the unconscious awareness of the connectedness and unity of all existence through the spiritual experience. Moreover, it must have remained so for many thousands of years, notwithstanding the advent of reflective awareness in the expansion of language, until patriarchality began to destroy or to obscure the unconscious awareness of the connectedness of all existence. The biology of love, through the acceptance of the legitimacy of everything, must have constituted for our ancestors the emotional opening for seeing all, and, therefore, for the expansion of their operational knowledge and understanding of the world that they lived. At the origin of humanness, the expansion of the biology of love must have constituted the operational fundament that permitted our ancestors to see and to use analogical relations for the explanation of their existence as active components of a dynamic interconnected whole.

Patriarchality has altered all this, but not fully. Because the biology of love and intimacy is what makes the spiritual experience possible as an expansion of the awareness of the unity of all existence, and the biology of love and intimacy is still a fundamental aspect of human life, it is still possible to regain the expansion of awareness of the unity of all existence as a spontaneous feature of human daily living. Thus, even now, in our present manipulative Western patriarchal culture with its essentially non-spiritual character, we still see "being in love" and the sexual intimacy that this entails as a fundamental source of spiritual experience. And not only that. We still see from the darkness of our patriarchal culture, that being in love is, through the extension of sensuality that it entails, our basic opening for a shift in our psychic existence towards the expansion of our intelligence and understanding as members of the biosphere. Furthermore, we think that the biology of love and intimacy constitutes our only possibility of reaching awareness of our inclusion and participation in the unity of the biosphere in a non-manipulative relation.

The Rupture of Intimacy

Nothing that we live in our psychic human existence is trivial. We can live many illusions, or many different virtual realities, as illusions are now frequently called; we can even know that we are living an illusion or a virtual reality as we live it, but our psychic existence is never an illusion or virtual regardless of how it arises. As our humanness occurs in the relational space as a psychic existence, it is what we live in our psychic existence that guides the transformations of our bodyhoods in our relational living, and we become in our bodies according to what we live in the interplay of our reason and our emotions in our conscious and unconscious being.

Much has been done in the technology of virtual realities under the argument that it contributes to the expansion and enrichment of human experience. Indeed, in the domain of technology virtual and non-virtual realities are forever an open field in which whatever is imagined in a manner that respects the structural coherences of the domain in which what is imagined is supposed to occur can be done. At the same time, much has been done in the domains of organ and tissue transplants, as well as in the cloning of tissues, organs or whole organism, which are practices that can be expanded immensely. Similarly, the domain of artificial expansion or supplementation of many of our body capacities through the design of mechanical, chemical, and electronic prostheses is also open-ended. And finally, the domain of genetic manipulations is now also open to unlimited expansion through genetic engineering. But in doing all this, will humanness be conserved or lost? All that we human beings can imagine as manipulations or artificial modifications of the bodies of animals and plants can be realized if we respect some fundamental cellular features in them. But what will happen to our human and individual identities if our brains are manipulated through tissue grafting or microcircuit implantation? How much can the body structure be changed and the human identity or the particular personal identities still be conserved? What happens to our psychic existence as we do all that to others or to ourselves? Or, for that matter, what is happening in our psychic existence so that we humans want to do those manipulations in the patriarchal mercantile culture that we presently live, and are willing to do so mostly without concern for the consequences of what we do in our own lives or in the lives of others?

The identity, the particular manner of being of any system (of any composite entity) as it exists as a particular totality in a given domain of interactions, has no intrinsic transcendental nature. That is, the identity of a system takes place and is conserved as a relational dynamics between the structure of the system and its manner of being in its domain of interactions and relations, and is, therefore, systemic. Or, in other words, the identity of a particular system is constituted and conserved in a recursive systemic dynamics in which the flow of relations and interactions of the structure of the system and the circumstances in which it exists contribute to realize and conserve it. Accordingly, the identity of any system lasts only as long as the systemic dynamics that defines and conserves it is indeed conserved through the structural changes that it undergoes. What we have said, of course, applies to all systems, but we are talking here of living systems in general and of persons in particular (see Appendix 2). It follows, as we have already said, that the identity of a living system, or of a human being, is not in its bodyhood, even though we recognize any particular individual being by observing or distinguishing certain features of its structure. Moreover, it is not the case that any structure can realize any particular identity, because there is an operational generative pairing between a structure and the relational dynamics to which it can give rise, and, therefore, between a structure and the identity that can be realized and conserved through it in a particular relational dynamics. So the structure, the bodyhood of a human being can change and its identity as such be conserved up to a point that becomes apparent when the observer sees that the relational dynamics that constitutes the identity we now know as "human being" is no longer there. It is through understanding this dynamics that we claim that humanness will be lost when the biology of intimacy and the biology of love are lost in the upbringing of our children.

The biology of intimacy and the biology of love are fundamental in human life: we are loving animals as a result of the biological and cultural evolutionary history that gave rise to us. The well-being that arises in living in the body nearness and in the acceptance of the body nearness of another in the pleasure of that nearness in total trust, as well as the well-being that arises in the sensual enjoyment of coexisting in mutual care solely for the pleasure of it, and not for whatever advantages such nearness may bring, are necessary for human physiological and spiritual well-being and harmony. Our patriarchal culture, through its psychic grounding in the emotioning of mistrust and control, as well as of manipulation and appropriation, has led us to accept political ideologies and economic theories that treat all human relations as political, manipulative, and economic transactions, as if the desire for power or gains in the domain of personal advantages were the biological primary motives in human relations and interactions. Moreover, by accepting such theories and political and economic ideologies, we live our interpersonal relations as if such theories indeed represented the fundaments of human life. But not only that. In the psychic space in which we live by accepting such ideologies and theories we visualize and treat all the processes of the biosphere as if they were occurring under considerations of gains and losses, utility and value, advantages and disadvantages in a temporal dynamics with past and future. Yet, as we attempt to explain and to understand all biological processes in those terms by introducing those notions in our descriptions as if they represented actual features of their operation, we become blind to the fact that biological processes occur in the present, not in the future or the past, and we only see what the political ideologies and economic theories, say. If we relate with another living being, human or not, whatever the dimensions of our relations, as if these were economic transactions, we do not see it, him, or her, we only see what we expect to receive or gain in a dynamics of power and control. As we do that, we become blind, deaf, mute, and so forth, with respect to the other, and intimacy is lost; human coexistence becomes a source of reciprocal use, manipulation, and abuse. When that happens, community life stops being social and becomes political.

The biology of love, the manner of living with the other in the doings or behaviors through which the other arises as a legitimate other in coexistence with oneself, and in which we human beings take total responsibility for our emotions and for our rational doings, is not a coexistence in appropriation, control, or demand. As the structural dynamics of the organism that brings about the behavior through which the other arises as legitimate other in coexistence with itself, love is the emotion that makes and constitutes that manner of living a social life in those relational dimensions. As such, the biology of love is the biology of mutual trust, and it makes possible the biology of intimacy as a particular expansion of social coexistence. Patriarchality through mistrust and control, through manipulation and appropriation, through domination and submission, interferes with the biology of love, pushing human relations away from the domain of collaboration and mutual respect towards the domain of political alliances, mutual manipulation, and mutual abuse. And as the biology of love is interfered with in our lives, our social life comes to an end; we become blind, deaf, mute, and unreachable with respect to our children, and we instrumentalize them for the perpetuation of our alienation in mistrust, manipulation, and control, in a life of mutual negation. What will happen to humanness under these conditions?

This is not a trivial concern. With the loss of collaboration in the loss of mutual trust and mutual respect, political relations prevail, and the acceptance of the legitimacy of the manipulation of the biosphere in general, and of the human life in particular, becomes the norm in the service of technology though the blindness of non-systemic thinking. Does it matter? If technology becomes the most fundamental and central feature of human endeavors, then indeed it does not matter that in the technological expansion and complication of human activities human beingness as *Homo sapiens-amans* should be lost to be replaced by the conservation of some new being like *Homo sapiens aggressans*, or *Homo sapiens arrogans*, for example. The conservation of some new *Homo sapiens* identities will change the course of history, and human beingness as *Homo sapiens-amans* shall disappear, or it will remain hidden in some distant pockets of primitive life. Poets of science fiction have played already with this idea. But, if loving humanness remains important and valuable for us as human beings, then technology will not determine human life, and the biology of intimacy will not be lost or destroyed but will be conserved. If this happens, the biology of love, together with the biology of intimacy, will continue to be the source and the fundament of the psychic identity of our descendants as human beings of the *Homo sapiens-amans* kind. But, how can that happen?

Conservation of Humanness

The biosphere does not care about human existence in general or about our existence as loving human beings in particular. Nor does the earth or the cosmos care. It is only us *Homo sapiens-amans* who care, or can care about humanness, or about the biosphere, or about the earth as our living space as loving human beings. And we shall care only as long as we conserve our loving humanness by living in care for ourselves and other living beings in the biology of love, because that is what makes us loving human beings. But as we are now living in a patriarchal culture that does not conserve this manner of living, how can we conserve loving humanness? We answer: by living in the biology of love, being aware that the biology of love is conserved through living in the biology of love. But how can we do that?

We know that the invitation to conserve loving humanness by living in the biology of love appears difficult to follow because it does not seem to say what to do. But we humans do know what to do because we are loving *Homo sapiens-amans* . . . still. We have said many times that love is the domain of those relational behaviors through which another arises as a legitimate other in coexistence with oneself. When we behave in love, the other does not need to justify his or her existence in relation to us, nor do we demand anything from him or her even when we ask him or her to do something for us. In the biology of love disagreements are openings for the expansion of a conversation, not sources of mutual denial, even when one is aware that coexistence with the other requires that one or the other should change his or her doings. In the biology of love, disagreements are opportunities for the initiation of responsible concerted actions. We know this because even in the midst of our manipulative patriarchal culture we still live the biology of love in friendship, and friendship as a domain of relational behaviors in trust occurs in the biology of love. Or, we know how to live in the biology of love because we were lucky enough to live in it in our early childhood even in the midst of our patriarchal culture because we were born in an undistorted mother/child relation of loving care, or because there was at least one adult that related with us in the biology of love. Indeed, we still have the capacity to live in the biology of love if we release our cultural addiction to the patriarchal demands of mistrust, control, power, domination, or abuse, because the aggressive world that these emotions entail is not our basic biological world, and as we release those additions the biology of love reappears spontaneously.

Indeed, we know from our babyhood how to be in the biology of love because love is our biological starting point. We are born in love, that is, in the implicit trust that there is a loving world open to receive us, and not in helplessness or defenselessness in an aggressive world. Thus, a new born baby seems to say: "Here I am, a loving being, and I can become a loving human being all my life if you love me." We humans are not unique in this; all living beings live in the implicit trust that the world is there for them as a paradise that will provide them with everything for living. But we are special because we belong to an *evolutionary history of neoteny* in the expansion of love and intelligence. Moreover, as we human beings are loving neotenic animals, love can be cultivated or denied in us, but it does not need to be taught. Love is the biological fundament of our humanness, and we could not be taught to love if we did not have the biology for it. So we know how to cultivate love if we just accept the biology of love because love is our natural manner of being in our biological fundament. Yet, even though we are biologically loving animals, the manner of living as loving human beings is a systemic condition that either is realized and conserved systemically, or is lost as it is not cultivated and becomes replaced by the systemic conservation of another manner of living that is centered in some other emotion.

We claim that humanity's present problem (that is, a problem as long as we still care for loving humanness because love is still part of our living) is that we have so much denied love as a constitutive feature of our humanness through our patriarchal living in competition, abuse, and aggression that we have almost forgotten how to cultivate it as a daily aspect of our existence. And in these circumstances we feel at loss, as if we were deprived of something that we do not know any more how to recover because we do not know how to recognize it, and we do not know how it should be taught, or even if it can be taught. The biology of love, though, is not something that has to be taught because it is still the innate biological fundament of every new born human child. Indeed it cannot be taught explicitly, as if it were some specific behaviour or value. Rather, the biology of love can only be cultivated as its existence can only be realized systemically in the epigenesis of a living human being. Love can only be cultivated or denied, and it can only be cultivated by living it.

The biology of love is a systemic relational dynamics that can be cultivated by living in a loving relational domain, or it can be actively denied by living in aggression and arrogance, but it could not be created if it were not already a basic aspect of our biology. Therefore, if we want our children to become socially well integrated self-respecting adults, who conserve their *Homo sapiens-amans* identity as a matter of course, we must cultivate in them this identity by living with them in the biology of love from the earliest moments of their lives, indeed beginning as we accept them as our children in the mother's womb (Verden-Zöller in Maturana and Verden-Zöller, 1993.)

In the biological and cultural evolutionary history that gave origin to us, the conservation of the biology of love has been a spontaneous systemic process because in our ancestors daily life, it was realized as a coexistence in mutual acceptance and care as a feature of the defining manner of living of their lineage. The biology of love was the actual daily living that gave origin to us as the particular kind of bipedal primates that we are. Now our daily life even in our childhood is frequently not so, or is becoming not so, because in the emotioning of our Western patriarchal culture we are under a continuous pressure for becoming more and more manipulative, political, technological and commercial, in all aspects of coexistence, including in the mother/child relation and the educational child upbringing.

If we indeed want our lineage of loving human beings to continue to exist we must recover the mother/child relation as a relation of total trust in mutual body acceptance in free play as a feature of early childhood as well as in the later upbringing of the child. And we must do so by creating the operational psychic dynamics of a daily life that makes it possible for the mother/child relation as a relation of mutual care and respect to be spontaneously realized in the *Homo sapiens-amans* manner of living as a cultural living that involves our whole life. That is, if we want to recover the mother/child relation as a relation in mutual respect in total body acceptance, playfulness, and in the joy of doing things together, we must create the psychic relational space in the life of the community, including both males and females, that makes that naturally possible. Yet, for that to happen, however, commercial and political living must be expelled from the domain of childhood and early youth. If we want our children to grow as self-accepting, self-respecting, socially well-integrated, responsible adults, then living in the biology of love must be conserved through adulthood by offering to our children as they grow the full possibility of a coexistence honestly centered in self- and social respect, cooperation, and responsibility as natural manners of living by living with them in the biology of love. Loving human beingness is culturally conserved as a spontaneous human living if we live in the biology of love. But now, in our historical present, we are culturally denying our spontaneous living in the biology of love, and loving human beingness can only be recovered and conserved intentionally through the protection of the *amans* aspect in the upbringing of our children.

Loss of Innocence

We have said that humanness arose as our ancestors began to live in languaging as a manner of living conserved generation after generation through the learning of their children. Moreover, we can infer from our present condition as talking animals, that languaging in our ancestors must have begun by involving the production of mouth-modulated sounds that allowed at least in principle for endless recursions in the consensual coordinations of consensual coordinations of behaviors and emotions of a daily life lived in the biology of love and intimacy. And we think that it must have been so because our ancestors, as they began to be savannah dwellers, must have produced mouth sounds in their coordinations of behaviors as they moved in interconnected small bands, perhaps much like quails do today,. Indeed, we think that humanness must have begun in the conservation by children generation after generation of oral and gestural conversations that constituted from the very beginning oral cultures as closed networks of oral and gestural conversations that coordinated the emotionings and doings of daily life.

When our ancestors began to live in conversations, they must have lived their daily lives immersed in the natural coherences of a cosmic spiritual existence as a matter of course. Only much later in the flow of their cultural history, when they began to reflect about themselves and the world they lived in their daily living, would our ancestors have begun to see their inclusion in a network of being that could be described but which was not questionable, and which until then had been lived a matter of course. That this must have been so is still apparent in the daily life and the mythical traditions of oral cultures, which show that in these cultures human beings still implicitly or explicitly treat themselves as integral components of a spiritual cosmos, particularly if they have not been transformed through the influence of our western patriarchal thinking. In oral cultures the awareness of the doings and emotionings that comprise daily life in the here and now are a central aspect of their fundamentally spiritual existence. In this living, they created goddesses and gods as aspects of their psychic existence who operated both as evocative concretizations of the human participation in the natural flow of the cosmic coherences of daily life, and as mystical instruments for the conservation of the awareness of that participation. Accordingly, in oral cultures the problems and difficulties that arise in the daily life of a community were lived as revealing a loss of awareness of the human participation in the cosmic coherences of all existence, and ceremonies and rituals were performed involving those goddesses and gods through the mystical reenacting of that participation with the purpose of recovering that awareness, or of conserving it if it had not been lost.

As languaging beings, we humans are rational animals. That is, we operate in our languaging according to the coherences of the different domains of consensual coordinations of consensual coordinations of behaviors that we generate as the different domains of existence that we live. In oral cultures rationality occurs as a matter of course as it is lived through a languaging that takes place involving the immediate operational coherences of a daily life lived without distance between arguments and emotions. As a result, in oral cultures rationality is a blending of analogical and local causal thinking based on the expansion of the coherences of the daily life. In these circumstances, when in the flow of coexistence questions arise that demand an explanation of all that exists, rational arguments and emotions become separated from the doings of daily life, and arguments become mainly analogical in the creation of a mythical history. In our Western patriarchal culture, rationality has acquired a different character.

Oral cultures are basically trustful of the fundamental goodness of a living cosmos that includes humans. In these cultures life takes place in the present, as a matter of course, and people live with a sense of being included in the coherences of life. But we modern human beings do not live now trusting our inclusion in the spontaneous and coherent dynamics of a systemic cosmic existence of which we are a constitutive integral part, and in our lack of confidence we want to control everything. Indeed, as we have already said, in our Western cultural history patriarchy introduced mistrust and political manipulation into our daily life as part of a continuous and pervading search for certainty in the course of human existence, both by means of a direct control of human life and through the attempt to control what is seen as an *opposing and aggressive nature*. In this process, local causal reasoning has become the declared main manner of thinking in our Western culture, giving to it an orientation that denies emotions in general, and love in particular, as the fundaments of our humanness as rational beings. This is so even in our new domains of existence as we live in the recursive dynamics of languaging in a way progressively more distant from the immediate coherences of daily biological living.

Moreover, in this mood of local causal thinking and the negation of love as a fundament of human existence, technology has expanded its daily presence in our imagination and in the operationality of our daily living to such an extent that we not only depend on it to conserve our modern human life, but we also have come to believe that through it we can control everything, including problems of human coexistence. But human problems are emotional, not rational or technological; they arise when in a person or in a community there are conflicting desires that lead to opposite actions, not when there is a rational or technological inconsistency. Therefore, rationality or technology cannot solve human problems; their solutions are emotional and arise when the various desires in the person or in the community stop leading to opposing actions. This is so even when rationality or technology permits us to generate some relational instrument with which we may expand our vision, change perspective, or bridge operational domains in a way that helps us to change our emotions.

Our ancestors in non-patriarchal cultures lived in a systemic dynamic interconnectedness within a cosmos that they were aware of and able to integrate. And as they lived their cosmic interconnectedness, they lived it in a systemic thinking of multidimensional coherences that they knew how to evoke but could not describe in detail. In that way of living they were not concerned with controlling the different aspects of their existence. They just lived them; and they did so through the conservation of practices that both conserved and realized their harmonious participation in the cosmic dynamics of their daily living in the human community to which they belonged. By living in such a manner a child did not have difficulty in growing up as a socially integrated self-respecting individual implicitly operating as part of a whole. Indeed, in his or her doings as a member of the community, he or she learned the coherences of daily life as a network of reasonings, emotionings, and doings that conserved his or her human beingness. To the extent that trust was the central mood in an oral culture, controlling was not the emotioning that defined its manner of living.

In the Western patriarchal culture that we presently live, mistrust is the central mood that guides our relations, and control is the grounding action of our daily living in a linear, non-systemic, thinking of cause and effect. But local linear thinking, when lived as the basic manner of thinking, destroys systemic understanding, separating us from daily living because we no longer fully grasp the systemic coherences of the world we live through living it in its daily coherences. And we have to learn the systemic coherences of the world that we live by explaining them. As we live mostly in explanations, we think that we learn the systemic coherences of our domain of existence as we explain them with the secret hope of opening dimensions for their manipulation and control. In the domain of human relations this has disruptive consequences because it destroys the multidimensionality of the other by separating us from the systemic coherences present in the immediacy of daily life by breaking it into different steps of control. Such manner of living destroys or negates the biology of love.

As a result, we no longer know what happens with our children as they grow socially disconnected in a meaningless coexistence, or as they become unhappy beings with no sense of participation in the world in which they are supposed to be. Nor do we see that we depersonalize them as we project them to a future that is supposed to fulfill our desires, not theirs. Moreover, by being deluded and enchanted with the power of local linear thinking because of its the expansion of our capabilities for technological design and the promise of control of human relations that it seems to offer, we create around our children a psychic space that continuously negates them in the negation of the biology of love. So our children choose to search for their own presence in the present moment through drugs, gangs, or despair. They have lost innocence because they no longer trust.

We modern human beings are emotional animals alienated by the belief that patriarchal local linear thinking allows us to explain and control everything in a linear causal manner, taking us beyond our unreliable emotional nature while expanding our understanding of ourselves. But linear causal thinking does not by itself lead to the expansion of our understanding in general, nor of the understanding of ourselves in particular. Indeed, the understanding of ourselves as human beings requires both systemic analogical and local linear causal thinking. Understanding occurs as we place our knowledge in a wider context that gives it connectedness to a network of systemic relations. Understanding arises in an operation in the emotional domain that releases our hold on our local linear thinking.

Emotions constitute the relational grounding on which we live every instant of our life, and all our reasoning and all the rational systems that we develop stand on basic premises that we accept *a priori* as expressions of our desires or preferences in the flow of our emotioning. Moreover, depending on how we find ourselves in our emotioning we can be systemic or linear in our reasoning and thinking. In our systemic thinking we grasp the coherences of our inclusion in the biosphere and cosmos, and we operate according to the configurations of relations that we abstract consciously and unconsciously from the coherences of our living. But in our systemic thinking we do not see the local concatenations that constitute the network of systemic relations in which we make our systemic abstractions, and although we can distinguish them, we do not understand how they arise. In our local linear thinking we analyze networks of systemic relations in our living that we do not see or recognize as such, and decompose them in local linear pieces that appear to us in their locality to reveal the causal fundaments of the processes of our existence, obscuring their systemic coherences. These two manners of thinking have different presence in our daily life according to how we live our emotioning, and we speak of wisdom when we live them in an integrated manner. The operation of understanding requires both (see Appendix 5.)

With our present understanding of the biology of love we are now becoming aware that the source of our difficulties in our Western patriarchal culture is that because of our all-pervading desire for control, we have become alienated by the seduction of the effectiveness of local linear thinking in the domain of design. Through that alienation we have become greatly blind to the presence and the need for systemic analogical thinking for the understanding of living beings in general, and of our living as human beings in particular. Moreover, in our blindness we do not see that it is this blindness that constitutes our difficulty in the conservation of loving humanness because we do not see that the biology of love is the biological operational foundation of humanness, nor do we see that control destroys the biology of love and intimacy. But even given this alienation, the fundamental emotional need for the biology of love is so present in us that we still yearn for it in our daily life, and as long as this is so we are not totally lost and we can still attempt to conserve loving humanness. Since we are yet not totally alienated, we still can integrate systemic and linear rationality through a change in attitude if we release our desire for control, and in doing so we could conserve loving humanness in awareness that the biology of love and intimacy is our fundament. That, indeed, would be a cultural change of no little magnitude.

Our Cultural Existence

We claim that what one distinguishes when distinguishing a culture is a closed network of conversations as a closed network of coordinations of languaging and emotioning. This why we say that a culture is a closed network of conversations, and different cultures are different closed networks of conversations systemically conserved through their actual realization in the living of a collection of languaging beings. As such, different cultures are different manners of living as different networks of emotionings and doings that conserve different relational identities in the languaging beings that realize them. Due to its systemic character, a culture is both the realization of a manner of living and the medium in which the languaging beings that realize it live. So a culture is both the medium of realization of the living of the organisms that live it, and the actual interrelational living of those same organisms. Thus a culture constitutes the multidimensional conscious and unconscious psychic relational space in which the languaging beings who realize it live and become members of it. When a culture is not conserved, due to its systemic historical nature it disappears without any possibility of recovery, and the kind of beingness generated and conserved in its realization also disappears.

Due to the systemic conservation of the manner of living or ontogenic phenotype, and because cultural living is a feature of the ontogenic phenotype of languaging beings like us, our cultural living is our manner of conservation of our organic identity, and our cultural realization is part of the conservation of our human biological identity. Accordingly, we human beings are systemic beings who have arisen and are realized and conserved culturally in such a way that the structural dynamics of our bodyhood, our physiology, our genetics, and the psychic relational space that we live has arisen through the systemic cultural conservation of the biology of love and intimacy along the evolutionary history of the languaging bipedal primate lineage to which we humans belong. As evolution follows the path of conservation of manners of living and of variations on the manners of living already conserved, and not the path of conservation of the genetic constitutions or their variations, evolution follows the course of what remains systemically conserved (physiologically, anatomically, and genetically) generation after generation through the realization of each conserved variation of the manner of living conserved in the constitution of lineages. In other words, as a new lineage arises, it does so systemically co-opting all genetic variations under the realization of those features of the manner of living that define it, or the lineage disappears. And this is so because genetic variation constitutes the possibility for variations in the epigenetic courses lived by the members of a lineage, and hence, for new manner of living that, if they were in their turn also to be systemically conserved through reproduction, would give rise to variations in the original lineage, or to some new lineage altogether. In these circumstances, in the evolutionary history of a lineage the phylogenic drift of the genotype follows the phylogenic drift of the manners of living (or ontogenic phenotype) conserved in the systemic conservation of the lineage.

This has happened and happens in the evolutionary phylogenic drift of our *Homo sapiens-amans* lineage as in any other lineage. It is because of this that it is always possible that the systemic conservation of aggression as a cultural manner of living may result in a path of genetic drift that facilitates the conservation of aggression as an adult manner of living. Or, said directly, if living in aggression were to be culturally conserved long enough, then the transformation, realization, and conservation of the world which arises through that manner of living in interplay with the genetic drift brought about by that manner of living, could result in the arising of a new lineage that branches off the *Homo sapiens-amans* lineage, or replaces it, following a different evolutionary path. Indeed, as it is the manner of living culturally conserved that defines the course of human evolution, it is possible that in many occasions along the course of human history several different *Homo* lineages have coexisted at any time, and that one of them is now *Homo sapiens-aggressans* (see also Bunnell, 1997).

We human animals no doubt have the genetic constitution that permits us to develop, to live, and to culturally conserve arrogance and aggression as a manner of living, so that the whole world that we live becomes transformed accordingly, but it was not arrogance and aggression that defined the evolutionary trend that gave origin to us human beings. Love was the emotion that from the beginning constituted the core of the manner of living that defined our lineage. Yes, arrogance, aggression, greediness, violence, abuse, mistrust, indifference, and so forth can be culturally cultivated as manners of living, and give rise to a new *Homo sapiens* lineage, as well as to the world congruent with it that that manner of living generates. Indeed, any manner of living that does not kill the *Homo sapiens* being that we are before it is systemically reproduced through being lived by its children, can give origin to a new culture and to a new biological lineage.

Our Choice

So far, arrogance, aggression, mistrust, violence, greediness, and indifference to the other are only circumstantial cultural alienations in our human manner of living. But for how long? Their cultural cultivation and conservation may eventually result in the loss of loving human beingness as arrogance, aggression, abuse, violence, and indifference to other human beings and the biosphere become the basic guiding emotions in an evolutionary history centered in the systemic cultural conservation of the denial of the biology of love. We can do nothing that our genetic constitution does not permit, but our genetic constitution does not specify what we will do or what will happen to us along our lives, nor what genetic constitution will be conserved in the flow of generations. What we do along our lives or what happens in us along our living arises in an epigenetic manner in the contingencies of our daily interactions in the world that we create through our living. Genetics does not determine us, but it is a central aspect of what makes us possible as biological beings. In these circumstances, it is because we are biologically loving animals that we become ill and disappear as loving human beings in the denial of the biology of love.

Accordingly, if we want to conserve loving humanness, we have to conserve the biology of love culturally (in our epigenesis), and to do that we have to conserve culturally the conditions under which our children may grow naturally as self-respecting, socially conscious, courageous, honest, intelligent, and responsible loving human beings. And to do so, we, the now living human adults, must generate through our daily living the psychic relational space of the biology of love around our children as the cultural psychic space in which they become adults. Living in hypocrisy, pretense, and appearances, will not free us from such a responsibility if we want to conserve loving humanness. Due to their *Homo sapiens-amans* biology, human children grow, one could say, as experts in detecting emotions and emotional contradictions, so that they discover immediately our emotional lies, and when they do so, trust disappears, social life begins to be eroded and eventually disintegrates. Honesty is necessary for self-respect and mutual trust, and therefore, for social life to occur. Indeed, although the biological fundaments that constitute the possibility for our loving humanness are genetic, our realization as such in our anatomy, our physiology, and our behavior is cultural, and loving humanness must be lived culturally for our *Homo sapiens-amans* biology (genetics, anatomy and physiology) to be, in fact, systemically conserved in our biological evolution.

We human beings are loving animals even though we may become alienated through arrogance, aggression, greed, and violence, when we are exposed to a cultural living centered in arrogance, aggression, greed, and violence. Indeed, that we are loving animals is and will be our saving condition as human beings of the *sapiens-amans* lineage as long as we conserve the biology of love in our daily living. But, as we have just said, our humanness, like any other biological identity, is conserved in the conservation of the manner of living which defines it, and since our *sapiens-amans* identity is cultural and we live immersed in a patriarchal culture that denies the biology of love, we can go on being *Homo sapiens-amans* only if we want it. Only if we want to conserve our *Homo sapiens-amans* condition and live accordingly, will our *sapiens-amans* lineage be conserved. Only if we let our desire to conserve ourselves as *Homo sapiens-amans* become a conscious preference which guides our living by choosing at every moment love over control, and by choosing systemic understanding interlaced with linear thinking in care, over faith in technology and the design of human relations for the solution of our problems, only then will our *Homo sapiens-amans* condition be conserved because we live as such. Only if we prefer trust to mistrust, responsibility to hypocrisy, collaboration, sharing, and participation to greediness, power and obedience as we create the worlds that we create as we live as *sapiens-amans* human beings, only then will *Homo sapiens-amans* be conserved in our human biological and spiritual evolution (see Appendix 6.)

Final Comments

We have come to the end of this essay and we can deal now with the questions that we formulated at the very beginning. How is it that we care for the other? How is it that we have ethical concerns? How is it that most, if not all, human suffering arises through the negation of the biology of love, and is cured through its restitution? How is it that love is the first medicine? The answer that we have developed through this essay is that our humanness arose, and has been conserved through the living of our ancestors in the biology of love and intimacy, and that the biology of love and intimacy is the biological fundament of our concern for the other (of whatever kind, living and not living) for our ethical behavior, and for our physiological, relational and spiritual harmony.

Physiologically we are social love-dependent animals, so much so that we become ill and our social life at all ages is disrupted, when we are deprived of love. Physiological harmony is a systemic feature of the realization of the manner of living of an organism and does not take place as an aspect of the body dynamics totally independent of the interactions of the organism and the medium. All persons caring for the well-being of another know that this is indeed the case. What we do not usually know or fully understand, however, is the systemic dynamics involved in the physiology of an organism, and we do not usually know or understand this because through our belief in linear causality proper to our Western patriarchal culture, we generally do not learn to think systemically. Living in the biologies of love and intimacy as an interpersonal systemic relational dynamics takes place in us through the realization of our physiological systemic dynamics, and, accordingly, both our physiological and our relational dynamics take place systemically interrelated in such a way that if one is altered, the other is altered, too.

In these circumstances, values are abstractions that we make of our operation as social beings in the biology of love; therefore, values do not exist by or in themselves. Or, put in other words, values are declarations of intended or desired manners of human coexistence that we make because we care for the other. As such, values do not have compelling power by themselves, and this is why they have to be cultivated as aspects of the praxis of living if we want the actions that entail the desired manner of coexistence to be spontaneous aspects of our daily living. In these circumstances the biology of love is the fundament of all values, whatever their cultural form. It is the biology of love and the biology of intimacy that has made us the particular kind of bipedal primates that we are, human beings of the *amans* lineage, and it is the recursive conservation of the biologies of love and intimacy that makes the biological and cultural conservation of loving humanness possible. Furthermore, that this is so does not deny that we, as human beings, are cultural beings, but this does define the domain of cultural changes that we may undergo and still remain human beings of the *amans* kind. Any particular manner of being human is cultural. Modern patriarchy, with its contradictory demands for respect for human rights even in war (as was also the case in the Floral Wars of the Aztecs), is cultural. Values, as we have just said, are cultural; the self is cultural; meaning is cultural; and loving humanness as our biological manner of being is cultural—and is conserved or lost in the cultural cultivation or denial of the biology of love.

We humans can live and conserve any culture that does not kill us before its systemic reproduction and conservation in the learning of our children. This is the operational fundament for the history of cultural diversification of humanity. Furthermore, we humans can generate rational theories to justify all our desires whatever they may be. This has always been a feature of our human history, both explicitly and implicitly, but particularly during our European patriarchal history. In this culture we explicitly use reasoning to modulate our emotioning, unaware that in so doing we are also modulating our reasoning through our emotioning in a manner that furthers our alienation from the biology of love and intimacy that we learn as children. We are aware of this now, and aware that we are aware. What we do with our awareness of our awareness, is our basic responsibility in the present moment of our human history.

Calling attention to the grounding of values, ethics, and human beingness in the biology of love and intimacy is not to deny the cultural phenomenal domain as the domain of our human living through some sort of biological reductionism. Cultures are biological phenomena because they take place through the living of living system, but cultural phenomena take place in a domain of conversations, which is a different domain than the molecular domain of the realization of the living. Living takes place in the molecular dynamics that results in the constitution of molecular autopoietic systems, and cultures take place in the relational dynamics of language of the particular kind of molecular autopoietic beings who live in language. Our aim in this essay as we reflect on the biological grounding of our human cultural being has been to expand our understanding of the kind of living systems that we are as human beings in the relational domain, and to call into our awareness the realization that as such we are loving beings who depend on love for our existence because we belong to an evolutionary trend in the primate lineage in which love, and not aggression. has been the grounding emotion in our becoming humans. We also want to bring to the fore the awareness that this is so even though biologically we are capable of being alienated through aggression, arrogance, hate, abuse, violence, and torture, in relation to other living beings, human and not, and even to ourselves. Finally, our purpose in these reflections has also been to call into our awareness the awareness that when we live, or others around us live in violence, abuse, mistrust, arrogance, and mutual denial, we do not like it, and we become ill or do something to recover the biology of love in us or around us as our domain of existence. We think that the fact that we behave in this way reveals that as human beings we are love-dependent animals.

Still, a fundamental question remains that can be expressed in several forms:

- How is it that our conscious acceptance of our inclusion in the coherences of nature (the biosphere, the cosmos), something our ancestors did implicitly and unconsciously, expands our vision and systemic understanding?
- How can we accept our inclusion without being trapped in a linear thinking that we also want to use and not to deny?
- How does the biology of love in our realization as human beings expand our understanding of our inclusion in the biosphere and cosmos, whereas patriarchal causal linear local thinking under the desire for control and domination limits it?

We can answer these questions through the integration of systemic and causal linear local thinking that the reflections that we have made along this essay enable us to address.

Love, in the acceptance of the legitimacy of all existence, and in the trust that we are a natural part of this existence, opens us to grasp the coherences of the biosphere and the cosmos by letting us abstract these coherences from the coherences of our living without the restrictions of mistrust and the desire for control. In so doing, we abstract from the coherences of our living different kinds of regularities, and we live with them and through them formulating different kinds of laws that apply in the different domains of experiential coherences from which they were abstracted (Maturana, 2000). As that happens, we find ourselves being operational components of a historically systemic cosmos, rather than parts of a conglomerate of independent unrelated events. Our ancestors were aware of such interconnectedness as a feature of what they saw in their daily living, as they did not see themselves fundamentally different from other living beings. With that awareness, even if we mostly do not or cannot see the manner or form of interconnections of the different events in their local details, we can see their interdependencies as dynamic patterns of relations, and we can investigate those local details without becoming blind about the totality that they integrate. As our ancestors lived, seeing those patterns of interrelations without being blinded by the belief that local relations were everything, they could fully use their analogical rational thinking precisely because it was valid in the coherent historical dynamics to which they knew they belonged. Love is visionary, not blind, because it liberates intelligence and expands coexistence in cooperation as it expands the domain in which our nervous system operates. Love expands the domain in which our nervous system abstracts coherences from our living.

In patriarchal linear rational thinking, mistrust and the desire for control restrict the orientation of our gaze, and we see mainly local causal interconnections, greatly blinding ourselves to the systemic network of relations in which these occur. As a result, we put our attention mostly on the local causal connections to be found in the restricted domain that we believe gives us certainty for the control of the outcome of our actions by specifying that domain, and we essentially blind ourselves with respect to the systemic expanse that does not satisfy our expectations or in which that locality has a legitimate presence. The result of the desire for control, is that we want to know in order to design systems (situations, machines) that will give us certainty in the outcomes of our doings. The desire for control through linear rational thinking, which is the fundamental patriarchal alienation, blinds us, restricts our intelligence, and channels our coexistence and our doings into the limiting path of a continuous search for compelling arguments and for the fundaments of transcendental efficient actions.

Perhaps the beauty of our existence as human beings is that as we abstract the coherences of our living, we discover that they apply in an expanding domain of relations that permits us to see that we are part of a systemic biosphere and a systemic cosmos in which analogical and causal reasonings are both valid if we operate with them in the proper systemic understanding of where they apply. The operation of the nervous system as a detector of sensory effector correlations that arise at the sensory and effector surfaces of the organism in the flow of its encounters with its niche is what permits the organism to operate making distinctions of local and systemic relations in its domain of existence (see Appendix 6). In these circumstances, the systemic or local relations that an organism distinguishes in its living depends on the flow of its emotioning as emotions expand or restrict the dimensions of the encounter of the organism and the medium. Thus, the biology of love, through the operation in trust that it entails, opens our intelligence and expands our vision as components of the network of systemic coherences of the biosphere and cosmos that we integrate as living and languaging animals. As loving animals we human beings are particularly endowed with the ability to see and abstract features of those systemic coherences through our operation as participants in them, and as languaging beings we can use them in our explaining and understanding. But at the same time, patriarchal local causal thinking and reasoning, through the restrictive character of its subordination to the desire for control, restricts our view to local partialities in the network of systemic coherences to which we belong. Now, however, through our understanding of our fundaments in the biology of love, we can avoid the trap of the desire for control, and we can become free to integrate systemic and linear rational thinking as we have done in this essay. Furthermore, by doing so we become free to live the expansion of intelligence that the biology of love brings in us, as well as to realize the conservation of loving humanness in our daily life.

Chapter 5
Overview

At the beginning of this essay we proposed to present a manner of explaining, viewing, and understanding the constitution, origin, and conservation of loving humanness as the *Homo sapiens-amans* lineage of bipedal primates to which we belong. We have done this by showing the possible operation of neoteny and the biologies of love and intimacy in the establishment of our lineage and of our particular identity as human beings. In this process we have proposed that we human beings arose as sexual, sensual, and tender languaging bipedal primates, and that this is what we still are — so far. Furthermore by arguing about the origin of humanness in the biologies of love and intimacy, we have shown that human beings, like all living beings, are systemic entities that bring forth their world and conserve it as they live, by living as the kinds of beings that they are. Moreover, we have also argued that although we are languaging bipedal primates who live and exist in conversations, becoming human has not been the result of a history of fortunate genetic mutations properly selected, but rather the result of a history of systemic conservation of a manner of living realized and conserved through a systemic dynamics that co-opts all genetic variation that do not happen to deny its realization and conservation. Thus, we have argued that loving humanness is the result of a primate evolutionary history in the conservation of a manner of living that entails sexuality, sensuality and tenderness, entwined in the daily living in the biologies of love and intimacy. Loving humanness is, one could say poetically, a work of aesthetics as a life lived in a loving, easy coherence with the cosmos (biosphere) that makes such a life possible. Indeed, sensuality, tenderness, and sexuality, braided in a loving coexistence, are such basic features of our humanness that we have to invent rational and irrational arguments to manipulate our emotioning so that we may deny in our daily living any or all those human dimensions when we want power and control. And we manage to do so, barely surviving with some measure of social integrity in the patriarchal culture in which most of the human kind lives today, because we act as if we believed those arguments, even though we know them to be invalid. Because we know those arguments to be invalid in the unconscious dimensions of the psychic space that we learned in our childhood, now and then we find enough courage to respect our emotions, and we cautiously accept love as a basis for the reasoning that tells us that collaboration is closer to our intimate biological self than competition and aggression.

Now, and regardless of whatever else we may wish to do, to continue as *Homo sapiens-amans*, we must conserve our living as sensual, sexual, and tender loving beings in actual ecological coherence with the world that we bring about in our living. And, moreover, we have to do so while we are aware that the world we bring about, and with which we have to be in ecological and spiritual coherence, is one in which we are aware that we bring about the world that we live through our conscious and unconscious psychic existence, as we participate in the different conversations that we live. As we have said already, in the present moment of our cultural history, our *Homo sapiens-amans* identity must be lived as a desired work of human art, that is, as a product of the aesthetics of intentionally living as *Homo sapiens-amans*. We will remain *Homo sapiens-amans* only if we want to, because only then will we conserve the systemic dynamics that realizes and conserves this manner of living. Otherwise, we will disappear as *Homo sapiens-amans*, and a different lineage will replace us, while we just vanish in the flow of the biological and cultural evolutionary drift in which we live without even being aware of what is happening.

Perhaps other languaging bipedal primates that arose along with us as branchings of the *Homo* system of lineages have already disappeared because they did not conserve, as the center of their manner of living, sensuality, sexuality, and tenderness braided in a loving daily life of ecological coherence with themselves in the worlds they were bringing about. By not doing that, they may have destroyed themselves by endless strife, or they may have brought about their own destruction by facilitating ecological changes in which their manner of living could not be conserved. This may have happened while other *Homo* beings lived in cooperation rather than in competition for power and domination and thus managed to conserve as the fundaments of their living together the biology of love and intimacy in the changing world that they themselves were bringing about. Evolution, the process of natural drift, does not stop in any lineage unless that lineage comes to an end.

Vision, understanding, foresight, self-consciousness, and wisdom are features of a manner of living, not features of the physiological or anatomical constitution of an animal, even though they are possible through its physiological and anatomical constitution. The world that an animal, human or non-human, lives, arises as an expansion of its bodyhood as a space of (external and internal) relations generated through its sensory and effector correlations. Moreover, the world that we human beings live has relational features proper to our existing in conversations that can recursively generate endlessly different domains of realities that become co-opted as dimensions or parts of the world in which we realize our living. As a result of this systemic condition, our human existence is one in which we can live whatever world we bring about in our conversations, even if it is a world that finally destroys us as the kind of being that we are. Indeed, this has been our history since our origins as languaging beings; namely, a history of recursive creation of new domains of existence as different networks of conversations that entail different domains of distinctions, relational operations, and explanations (self-awareness, awareness of death, awareness of instruments, awareness of the public object, awareness of technology, and self consciousness). But it is also a result of our human history in our becoming reflecting, self-conscious, and self-aware beings, that it is only we who can, through our self-conscious intentional actions, change the course of the lives that we live. It is only we as self-conscious beings who can stop, if we so wish, any recursive unidirectional processes that we have generated, and that may have catastrophic consequences for the systemic dynamics of the flow of our own existence and the existence of other living beings in the biosphere. And this is so because it is only we who can act in the understanding of the systemic nature of all process in the biosphere, and it is only us who can desire not to destroy loving humanness because we like and respect our condition of being *Homo sapiens-amans*.

The cosmic structural drift occurs in a chaotic dynamics of continuous spontaneous structural changes in which local, dynamically stable situations of singular order arise from nothingness (no-thingness). In conversations about chaotic dynamics, such situations are called "strange attractors," but they are nothing more than the spontaneous constitution of singular dynamic entities through the conservations of dynamic relations. Those dynamic stable situations last as long as the conditions for their conservation take place, and when those conditions disappear, they disintegrate. Autopoiesis could be seen in this way, and one could say that autopoiesis is a strange attractor in a chaotic dynamics. The same could be said for any kind or species of living systems, for culture, or system of cultures. Indeed, any systemic singularity is an attractor that arises in an otherwise (structure-determined) chaotic dynamics. But pointing to that alone does not result in an expansion of our understanding of the domain of existence of any entity. The domain of existence of any entity is the domain of the relational dynamics in which it occurs and is conserved; and an entity is conserved as long as the relational dynamics that constitutes it is conserved. Moreover, as an observer distinguishes a system or entity, he or she makes an operation of distinction that implies the operation of the relations of constitution of the system or entity. One could say that the actual operation of a system or entity is what reveals it and the possibility of its description. The same happens with human beings who exist and are to be seen and understood in the relational domain that they generate and in which they are conserved through their operation as such. Or, in other words, it is in the domain in which we exist as loving human beings where what we do conserves or denies us as *Homo sapiens-amans*, and it is there where we can chose what to do. In general terms, whenever in a collection of elements a certain configuration of dynamic relations begins to be conserved, everything else becomes open to change (see Appendix 10). Therefore, we as human beings are not trapped in the destiny of an unconscious cosmos, even though we are part of it, precisely because we are self-conscious and it is because we are self-conscious parts of it that we can conserve loving humanness as a systemic dynamic identity by living as such. If we chose to live as *Homo sapiens-amans*, then loving humanness will be conserved, and everything else will change around its conservation.

We do not know whether or not there are other self-conscious beings in the cosmos that we bring about as we exist as self-conscious humans. It is most likely that there are, but as we are self-conscious beings, we realize the possibility and the operationality of self-consciousness in our cosmos. To say this is not vanity, but awareness of the peculiarity of our self-conscious loving human existence as biological systems. In many mystical traditions not distorted by the pretense of absolute transcendental knowledge, the spiritual experience is lived as an experience of identity with a loving and caring cosmic condition that pervades all existence. That this condition is frequently treated as representing an independent being usually called God, shows, we think, our care and awe in the face of the overwhelming character of such experience in our patriarchal culture. Yet, what is central in that experience is that it is an experience of love as the fundament of human existence.

No doubt speaking with the freedom of reflection as we have done in this essay may be taken as unscientific, as if matters such as love, ethics, and spiritual experiences were not biological phenomena. They are. In this essay we have not used any primary non-biological notions as an argument for what we have said, and in it love and ethics have appeared as features of our biological dynamics. We do not recommend love, but we say that without love as a biological phenomenon there is no social existence. There is no ethical imperative, but without ethics as a biological consequence of a human living in the biology of love, there is no *Homo sapiens-amans*.

Frederick Nietzsche wrote in *Thus Spake Zaratustra*: "God is dead". We prefer to think that we human beings of the *amans* lineage have fallen asleep; let us now awaken. We human beings are not gods, but we are *Homo sapiens-amans*, and we are aware now that our fundament is the biology of love and intimacy.

Appendix 1
Scientific Explanations

Science is a particular system of explanations of human experiences. Many scientists consider that science is a dialogue with nature, and that through that dialogue scientists find the laws that rule it. I think differently. I think that if one considers what a scientist does in fact, one finds that what a scientist does is explain his or her experiences as a human being in the way particular to scientific explanations. Furthermore, I find that in doing so a scientist does not explain the phenomena of an independent *reality*, but rather the domain of the experiences that he or she lives as a human being. As life happens to us, nature happens to us as all that we can live in the many different relational domains which we live as human beings. In what follows I shall not reflect on reality; I shall reflect on what we do as we make explanations.

One of the difficulties that is always present when one attempts to explain any experience is that of knowing when one has, in fact, explained what one wants to explain. With the awareness of this difficulty in mind, let me say a few words about explanations in general, and about scientific explanations in particular.

We learn at home during our early childhood as we live with our parents that an explanation is a particular kind of answer to a particular kind of question a question that asks how things, events, phenomena, or, in general terms, the experiences of the observer come about. Said more precisely, we learn in our childhood, although mostly unconsciously in the mere course of our living with our family, that an explanation is an answer to a question about the origin of some particular experience of the observer that is asked in such a way that it explicitly or implicitly demands an answer that satisfies the following two conditions:

1. The answer must consist in the proposition of a mechanism or process that, if it were allowed to operate, would give rise in the observer as a result of its operation to the experience that he or she wants to explain;

2. The generative mechanism or process proposed as an answer must be accepted as doing what it claims to do by an observer, who could be the same person that proposes it, because it satisfies some other condition that he or she puts in his or her listening.

When these two conditions are satisfied, the proposed generative mechanism or process becomes the explanation of the experience to be explained for the observer or observers who accept it.

There are three basic consequences to the fact that explanations must satisfy the two conditions indicated above. The first is that since an explanation consists in a generative mechanism accepted as giving rise to the experience (that is, phenomenon) explained as a consequence of its operation in a different operational domain than the one in which it takes place, explanations are not reductionist operations. Explanations do not consist in expressing the experience (phenomenon) that is to be explained in more fundamental terms (experiences or phenomena): *an explanation is the description of a generative mechanism that as a result of its operation gives rise to the phenomenon to be explained in a different phenomenal domain than the one in which it itself takes place.* The second consequence, is that explanations establish generative relations between phenomenal domains that do not intersect and are operationally independent. A generative relation is a constructive relation, not a deductive or inductive one. This means that one cannot deduce from the behavior of a whole what its composition is, and one has to decompose it if one wants to see how it is made. Similarly, it is for this same reason that one cannot deduce the whole just by looking at the components; one has to do the composing and then look at it. In order to understand a generative relation one needs a double look; one must look at the generative process and at its consequences independently because they happen in different non-intersecting phenomenal domains. The observer must look at the components in the domain in which they exist and at the whole in the domain in which it exists in order to see the generative relation that holds between them. The third consequence is that there are no explanations by themselves; explanations are interpersonal relations. A generative mechanism is not by itself an explanation of anything. A generative mechanism must be accepted by an observer as doing what it claims in the context of answering a question that demands an explanation as an answer to become in fact an explanation in the domain of experiences in which it is accepted.

But there is still an additional basic condition that must be brought in now. The observer does not accept or reject the proposed generative mechanism in a vacuum. *The observer accepts or rejects the generative mechanism proposed as an explanation according to whether it does or does not satisfy an additional condition that he or she puts in his or her listening. And this additional condition can be any.* In these circumstances, for an answer to the kind of question that demands an explanation as an answer to be in fact accepted as an answer, the explanation must fulfill two conditions:

1. It must have the form of a *generative mechanism* (I call this the *formal condition*); and
2. It must satisfy any additional condition put in his or her listening by the observer as an implicit or explicit condition of acceptance (I call this the *informal condition*).

The *informal condition* is usually not made explicit, so different observers may listen at the same time for different informal conditions even in situations where they seem to be in basic agreement. Indeed, the informal condition defines the kind of explanation that an observer wants and accepts. Due to these circumstances, unless the informal condition is made explicit, it is not possible to know what is accepted when somebody says that he or she accepts a particular generative mechanism as an explanation in answer to the kind of question that demands an explanation as an answer. This is so because one does not know the meaning of the act of acceptance. For this reason there are as many kinds of explanations as there are different kinds of informal conditions that an observer who wants to hear an explanation can put in his or her listening.

Scientific explanations are no different from explanations in general. What is particular to scientific explanations is the informal condition that scientists use. This is what gives scientific explanations their peculiar character and what specifies science as the particular kind of cognitive domain that it is. What is peculiar to scientists is that they have made the impeccable use of this particular informal condition their profession. I call the informal condition that we scientists put in our listening, and that we expect to be satisfied in order for us to accept a particular generative mechanism as a scientific explanation, the *criterion of validation of scientific explanations*.

This criterion consists of the coherent satisfaction of four operations that have to be directly or indirectly performed or accepted as properly done by the observer. These four operations are:

1. The description of what an observer must do to have the experience to be explained;

2. The proposition of a generative mechanism such that if it is allowed to operate, the result is that the observer has the experience to be explained in a different phenomenal domain than the one in which it takes place;

3. The deduction from all the operational coherences entailed in point 2 of other experiences that an observer could have, and of what operations he or she should do to have them; and

4. The realization by an observer of the operations deduced in point 3, and if he or she has the experiences

also deduced in that point, then and only then, point 2 becomes a scientific explanation. If after doing what is deduced in point 3 the observer does not have the experiences also deduced in it, the proposed generative mechanism must be abandoned and a new one must be considered.

I will now make a few comments about the criterion of validation of scientific explanations and about what we scientists do with it.

An observer is any person making distinctions. A scientist is any person that can satisfy the criterion of validation of scientific explanations and chooses to do so professionally. So science is the "club" comprising those persons who use the criterion of validation of scientific explanations to explain what they want to explain, and any particular science is a particular domain of statements validated through scientific explanations.

To do scientific explanations the observer does not require any assumption about an independent reality. Furthermore, in doing a scientific explanations an observer does not explain an independent reality, nor a world independent of what he or she does. Rather, an observer explains his or her world of experiences, and does so by using his or her experiences and the coherences among these experiences.

Although the aim of many scientists may be the prediction and eventual control of the events and happenings of the world in which we humans live, prediction and control do not enter as features of the criterion of validation of scientific explanations. When there is understanding, effective action is possible within the domain of operational coherences proper to the domain of understanding. If one is not aware of this, one may expect that science should allow for predictions of particular events that do not belong to the actual domain of validity of the scientific explanations with which one may pretend to validate those predictions. This is a frequent mistake as a result of insufficient understanding of the scientific domain in which one operates.

The criterion of validation of scientific explanations is the same criterion of validation that we use in daily life in a non-systematic manner. The difference between science and daily life rests in the fact that the scientist, as a person that lives under the passion of applying the criterion of validation of scientific explanations, is careful in not confusing domains when doing so, and is ready to abandon any accepted generative mechanism when the criterion of scientific explanations is no longer satisfied. It is because science permits us to explain human experience using human experience and the coherences of human experience, that science transforms human life. We change the world we live as we live it through science.

In a scientific explanation the observer chooses the experience to be explained from his or her domain of experiences as a poetic act of free imagination. The generative mechanism is also proposed by the observer in a poetic act, and it is specially designed by him or her using elements of his or her domain of experiences so that if it is allowed to operate it will give rise to the experience that he or she wants to explain also in the domain of his or her experiences.

Once a particular generative mechanism has been validated as a scientific explanation, it is treated as an experience (that is called fact) that can be henceforth used for the generation of new questions, or for use in the proposition of other ad hoc generative mechanisms in the explanation of other experiences

The power of scientific explanations to affect human life rests on the fact that they, like explanations in general, are manners of human coordinations of coordinations of behavior, and operate as such with the coherences of the human experiences, and only in the domain of human experiences in the realization of the human living. So the effectiveness of scientific explanations in human living is the result of the fact that they operate with the biological coherences of human living. This is valid even in the domain of physics to the extent that physics as a science is a domain of scientific explanations of the experiences of the observer as it operates in the particular experiential domain that scientists call physics.

As we explain we human beings use our experience and the coherence of our experiences to explain our experiences, and we do so while we call "experience" that which we distinguish as happening to us as we reflect on what we do or live. It is because of this that explanations do not deal with an independent reality, but are manners of interpersonal relations and deal, in fact, with the coordinations of our behavior in the flow of our coexistence with other human beings. What is significant in explanations in general, and particularly with scientific explanations, is that through them we human beings change our living, and in doing so, we change the world we live. The first two operations of the criterion of validation of scientific explanations are arbitrary, and in them resides the *poetics* of doing science because they arise as free expressions of the imagination, desires, or preferences of the observer. The other two operations, namely the deduction of new possible experiences and the realization by the observer of what he or she has to do to have those experiences, constitute the *engineering* of doing science. As a result, *as the first two operations of the criterion of validation of scientific explanations are specified as poetic acts, the other two become fixed, and what follows is strict deduction and structural design within the domain of experiences of the observer.*

My aim in the task of explaining and understanding cognition is not to explain or understand what we call reality in daily life, but to understand and explain all that we do and how we do it in the experience of our doing as we live the world that we live in our daily living as human beings. Because in explanations we as observers use our experiential coherences to propose generative mechanisms for our experiences, it does not matter that science should not be concerned with reality as we give a scientific explanation of the experience of cognition. With scientific explanations we explain the worlds that we live and how we live them, and we do so using the coherences of our living, even as we explain the world of knowing with our knowing.

Reality—that which we connote in our Western patriarchal culture when we speak of *reality*—is an explanatory assumption, an imagined domain of independent entities that we use in order to give a universal validity to our explanations of our experiences. But, if we become aware of the fact that the notion of *reality* is an explanatory proposition that does not enter as an argument in scientific explanations and is not required in these, we can become aware of the fact that what gives universal validity to scientific explanations is the application of the criterion of validation of scientific explanations. A scientific explanation is valid in any part of the cosmos or in any circumstance in which it is supported as such by the application of the criterion of validation of scientific explanations. Furthermore, as reality does not enter as an argument in the scientific explanations, its presence in the reflections of the observer is superfluous and irrelevant as long as he or she does not pretend to give intrinsic explanatory validity to it. But when the latter happens, human relations change, everything is distorted, and experiences such as perception, cognition, the manner of operation of the nervous system, the organization of the living, and the manner of conservation of the ontogenic phenotype through the flow of phylogenic drift in the history of living systems can neither be explained nor understood. But there is more. If we do not release our belief in an independent reality, science cannot be understood as a domain of explanations of the experiences of the observer with the coherences of experiences of the observer, and the relation of scientific explanations with life in general, and with the world that the observer as a cognitive being lives in particular, remains beyond any possible understanding. Furthermore, if we do not release our belief in an independent reality, we cannot understand that predictions of particular events do not belong to the domain of science but to the domain of design.

As we explain we see that we need, for epistemological reasons, an independent substratum that would give origin to our experiences as a result of its manner of operation. But at the same time, as we see and understand what we do as we explain, we also see and understand that we cannot say anything that may characterize such a substratum in itself. And finally, we also see that we cannot speak about such a substratum for two reasons: one is that even the notion of it does not apply because it is a notion proper to a domain of entities that are conceived as if they were independent from what the observer does; the other is that language is a manner of living together in coordinations of coordinations of behavior, and objects, notions, relations, and so forth are entities that arise in the flow of our recursive coordinations of behavior and do not refer to things or processes independent of what we do.

No doubt that as we describe our experiences in daily life we usually speak as if we were dealing with objective entities that belong to an independent reality. We do so by referring to our experiences in terms of things, entities, or relations as if they existed independently of what we do as we distinguish them. Thus, for example, if a friend suddenly appears, we may say: "My friend, where did you come from?" implying that we think that he or she existed prior to our distinction and that he or she came from a place which also had an independent existence.

As we explain our experiences with the coherences of our experiences, what we do is explain our doings with the coherences of our doings. As we remain in the domain of our doings as human beings all the things, entities, or relations that we bring forth in our distinctions arise as doings within the coherences of the domain of our doings as if they were indeed independent objective things, entities, or relations in the domain of our doings. In these circumstances we experience the sudden appearance of our friend as an objective independent event in a domain of reality that we brought forth as an aspect of our living through the coherences of our operation in the domain of our doings as human living systems. There is no difficulty with the use of the notion of reality in this situation unless we do not see or are not aware that the notion of independence of existence is an explanatory argument conceived to account for the repetitiveness of our experiences. If we are aware of the latter, we become aware also that we live in as many different domains of reality as we live different domains of experiential coherences. If we are not aware that we cannot validate what we say by claiming that we have a privileged access to an independent reality, we demand obedience in our relations and we become tyrants

Scientific explanations, and therefore science, is not a conceptual and operational instrument that permits us to handle a domain of independent objective entities, rather it is an operational and conceptual instrument that permits us to explain and understand what we do as human beings through our operation in the different domains of operational coherences in which we may live. It is because of these circumstances that in the use of science for the prediction or design of possible events the observer must always be careful to make his or her computations and designs without losing awareness of the domain of operational coherences in which the scientific explanations and scientific statements that he or she is using apply, and without losing sight of the fact that he or she is always dealing with human life.

Finally, there is great confusion about notions such as reality and existence, as we implicitly or explicitly treat them as concepts referring to things intrinsically independent from the observer. What I claim is that if one becomes aware that what one explains is experience, and that one uses the coherences of experiences, or the coherences of the coherences of experience to explain experience, one cannot avoid becoming aware that the notion of reality is an explanatory notion. Similarly with the notion of existence. If one becomes aware that what one explains is experience, and that one uses the coherences of experience, or the coherences of the coherences of experience to explain experience, one cannot avoid becoming aware that existence is a manner of referring to the condition of constitution of that which is distinguished, or to what must occur for something to have an operational presence in the cognitive domain of the observer. Thus, for example, electrons are explanatory notions, and they exist as long as the conditions that constitute them apply. This is why the observer expects that as long as those conditions occur, electrons will be there to show their operational presence. But at the same time, the conditions of existence of the electron can be talked about only as configurations of experiential coherences or configurations of coherences of experiential coherences of the observer.

No doubt for epistemological reasons one needs a substratum that makes possible that which the observer distinguishes, including the observer as he or she arises in self-distinction. But it is not possible to say anything about that substratum other than it permits what it permits in the domain of the living of a specific observer. If the observer lives in one way it brings forth an elephant; if he or she lives in another way, it brings forth an electron.

Appendix 2
Structural Determinism & Structural Intersections

Another difficulty that we usually have in fully understanding biological phenomena in general, and human phenomena in particular, is that we do not consistently follow in our explanations, our arguments, or our reflections, all the implications of the operationality of structural determinism.

As we argue, reflect, or explain in the praxis of daily life and in the praxis of science, we do so in the implicit and sometimes explicit understanding that systems operate according to how they are made through the operation of the properties of their components. Thus, if our car does not move when we press the accelerator, we do not go to the medical doctor to have our foot examined, we go instead to the mechanic and ask him or her to modify the structure of the car so that it will operate again according to our expectations. That is, we treat the car as a structure-determined system. If we become ill, we go to a medical doctor with the same request that we presented to the mechanic in relation to our car, and we ask him or her to examine our body (our structure) and to modify it if possible, so that we become healthy again. In other words, we treat ourselves also as structure-determined systems. In fact, in all that we do in our lives we deal with the coherences of our experiences, and we treat all the systems or entities that appear in our distinctions according to the operational regularities with which they arise in the coherences of our experiences; that is, we treat all systems as structure-determined systems. Moreover, we do this regardless of how we explain the regularities or coherences of our experiences.

Structural determinism, however, is not an explanatory principle or an a priori ontological assumption, it is an abstraction of the regularities of our living and of our operation as living systems as the regularities of our living appear in our reflections as coherences of our experiences. Or, said in other words, the notion of structural determinism arises as an abstraction of the coherences of the experiences that an observer lives, and this is why there are as many different domains of structural determinism in our explaining as there are different domains of operational coherences that we may live. In these circumstances, the so-called laws of nature are condensed or abstract expressions that we scientists use to connote without describing them in detail the regularities of our experiences, or the coherences of the coherences of our experiences that we use at any instant to explain other regularities of our experiences. Moreover, it is precisely because the notion of structural determinism arises as an abstraction of the coherences of the experiences that we live as we operate as human beings, that it can be used in scientific explanations, and scientific explanations can be and are effective in explaining and expanding our experiences. Finally, it is because the notion of structural determinism is an abstraction of the coherences of our living that we can use it in technological design to construct whatever we conceive or imagine in any domain of structural determinism, provided we operate within the operational coherences that define that domain.

In what follows I shall make explicit some of the basic relations that the notion of structural determinism connotes, and in doing so I shall speak in terms of entities and their relations because I am speaking of the coherences that we distinguish in our doings (experiences) as we operate as observers.

Structure-determined Systems

Structure-determined systems are systems, or composite entities, such that everything that happens in them or to them is determined in them at every instant by their structure and structural dynamics at that instant. External agents that may impinge upon a structure-determined system only trigger in it structural changes determined by its structure without specifying them. A structure-determined system, therefore, has a structure that changes following a course contingent on the course of its interactions, and whenever in the course of our living we see or live a situation that seems to violate structural determinism, we are astonished. Magic shows play with our trust in structural determinism by creating situations in which it appears to be violated but is not. If structural determinism seems to be violated in any circumstance of daily life, we immediately attempt to explain what happens by thinking that something is wrong in the sense that something different from what was expected is happening, that there is a fraud, that some one is cheating, or, in the extreme case, we resort to the notion of a miracle to express our astonishment.

Experience

I speak of experience as that which the observer distinguishes as happening to him or her in his or her living as a human being as he or she operates as such in language. Experiences are not of things or of reality, but they are that which the observer is aware of distinguishing as he or she operates as a languaging self-aware human being. As we operate as observers, we live the many different domains of experiential coherences that we live as many different domains of entities, objects, operations, or relations that we distinguish and treat as if they were independent entities. Each domain of experiential coherences that we live, however, arises in our operation as structure-determined systems, and it is not and cannot be deemed to exist independently of what we do. Not even we ourselves are entities independent of our operations of distinction, for we arise in our distinctions as we operate as observers in self-awareness.

Observer

The observer is any one of us, any human being as she or he operates in language making distinctions. Distinctions are operations that we perform in the domain of our experiences that result in our living (treating) one of those experiences as something independent from us. Accordingly, as we operate as observers we distinguish our experiences as entities of different kinds (objects, relations, processes, and so forth), and these entities arise in our distinction endowed with properties that also arise in our distinction as the dimensions through which we separate them from other entities and how we relate or interact with these. As we human beings operate as observers distinguishing whatever we distinguish, we distinguish through the operation of the properties with which they arise in our distinction two kinds of unities (entities); namely, simple and composite unities.

Simple and Composite Unities

A simple unity is an entity that, as it arises in our distinction, it arises as a totality (or whole) in which we cannot distinguish components, or in which we choose not to do so. Simple unities operate as totalities, and they operate as totalities through the realization of the properties with which they arise in the moment in which they are distinguished by the observer. As a result of their manner of origin, simple unities exist as totalities in the domains of relations and interactions defined by the operation of the properties with which they arise as such, as they are distinguished as such.

In contrast to a simple unity, a composite unity is an entity that an observer first distinguishes as a totality, and in which he or she then separates components. The components of a composite unity arise in its decomposition as those elements that when put together in a particular manner reconstitute the composite unity as a totality, giving origin to its properties as a totality in the relational and interactional domain in which it is distinguished as such. The components of a composite unity exist, then, only as the components integrate it as a totality in relations of composition, and not as independent entities. Therefore, it follows that as an observer distinguishes a simple unity he or she does so through interacting or relating with it in the domain of the operation of its properties as such. Conversely, as the observer distinguishes a composite unity he or she does so through interacting and relating with the unity distinguished both through the operation of its properties as a totality, and through the operation of the properties of its components.

In these circumstances a composite unity exists and operates as a matter of its constitution in two non-intersecting operational domains, namely:

1. in the domain in which it is distinguished as a totality or whole through the operation of the properties with which it arise as a simple unity as the observer interacts with it as such; and

2. in the domain in which the observer interacts with the elements that compose it as a composite entity as he or she distinguishes these by decomposing the composite entity.

But it is also the case, and it is not always fully seen, that a composite unity interacts as a totality through the operation of the properties of its components. That is, the relational and interactional domains in which a composite unity exists as a whole and, therefore, in which it interacts and relates as a totality exhibiting properties as a totality, arises as a result of its composition. Yet, as the observer distinguishes a composite unity as a totality, its components become invisible to him or her even though it interacts as a totality through them. The components of a composite unity appear only in the operation of decomposition that the observer performs upon it, and the observer must operate in the two domains of existence of the composite unity to see it both as a composite entity and as a whole.

Let us now consider an example. A couple arises as a simple unity (as a totality) in the moment in which two persons begin to move and behave with respect to each other as a couple, and it exists as a couple in the domain of relations where couples take place as social entities. At the same time, a couple arises as a composite entity in the domain in which the observer sees the persons who compose it as he or she interacts with them as individuals, while at the same time he or she recognizes them as the components of the couple that he or she has distinguished. Another example: a living system exists as a simple unity in the domain in which it relates and interacts as a totality or whole, and it exists as a composite unity in the domain of relations and interactions of the molecules that compose it as a molecular system. However, for the observer to see and understand the living being as a system (composite entity), he or she must be able to interact with the living system in its two domains of existence: the domain in which it is an organism, and the domain of its molecular components. And for the observer to be aware of his or her distinction, he or she must also operate in a third domain in which he or she sees his or her double distinction.

In summary; it is because a composite entity exists as a totality in a domain that arises de novo as a result of its composition, that a system as a composite entity exists and operates (interacts) in two phenomenal domains that do not intersect. Systems are composite entities, and they exist as such in two domains: in the domain in which they are totalities or wholes, and in the domain of operation of their components. And it is because systems are composite unities that systems interact in both domains through the operation of the properties of their components.

Organization and Structure

The configuration of relations between the components of a system that defines its class identity is the *organization* of the system. That is, a system exists as a system of a particular kind (has a particular class identity) only as long as its organization is conserved. An example: the configuration of relations between two persons that constitutes and defines them as a couple is the organization "couple," and therefore, a couple exists only as long as the organization couple is conserved in the relations and interactions of the two persons who constitute it. Similarly, the configuration of dynamic relations between molecules that defines a system as a living system (the organization "living system" or molecular autopoiesis) exists as long as the organization living system (molecular autopoiesis) is continuously realized in the dynamics of interactions and relations of the molecules that compose it. It follows that the conservation of the organization of a system is its condition of existence. In these circumstances, a system arises and exists as a whole of a particular kind in the moment in which the organization that defines it as such arises and begins to be conserved in the dynamics of relations and interactions of a collection of elements that become in that way its components. A system can exist only as long as the organization that defines and realizes it is conserved in the interactions and relations of its components.

The components plus the relations between them that at any instant realize a particular system as a system of a particular class constitute its *structure*. The structure of a system includes both components and relations between them, and therefore has more dimensions than its organization, as the organization entails only relations. Since the organization of a system is the configuration of relations between its components that define its class identity, it follows both that the organization of a system is a subset of the relations that form part of the structure of the system and that an organization does not exist independently of the structure of the system in which it is realized. At the same time, it also follows that the components of a system do not exist as such as independent entities. Elements become components of the system as they integrate and constitute its structure while participating in the relations of composition that realize it as a particular case of a particular class. If an element stops participating in the composition of a particular system, it stops being a component of that system and becomes either a free element or the component of another system. Components only exist through participating in a composition.

Domains of Structural Change

Just as the organization of a composite unity defines its class identity, a composite unity remains of the same class identity only as long as its organization remains invariant. Accordingly, the organization of a composite unity is necessarily an invariant as long as the composite unity conserves its class identity and vice versa — the class identity of a system remains invariant as long as its organization is conserved. Something different happens with the structure of a composite entity. The structure of a composite unity (system) may change either as a result of the internal dynamics of the system or through structural changes that are triggered in it by external agents that impinge upon it. In either case, the organization of the system may be conserved or it may be lost. If it is conserved the system changes its structure, but its identity as a particular case of a particular class is conserved. However, if the organization of the system is not conserved while its structure changes, the system disintegrates as a case of the original class and something else appears in its place. As a consequence, a structure-determined system can undergo four kinds of structural changes, namely:

1. Structural changes proper to the internal structural dynamics of the system and course in a way such that the system conserves its organization; I call these *changes of state*;

2. Structural changes proper to the internal structural dynamics of the system and course in a way such that the original organization of the system is lost and the

original system disintegrates; I call these *disintegrations*;

3. Structural changes that arise in the structural dynamics of the system triggered in it by external agents and that course in such a way that the original organization of the system is conserved; I call the interactions that trigger such structural changes in a system *perturbations*; and finally,

4. Structural changes that arise in the structural dynamics of the system triggered in it by external agents and that course in such a way that the original organization of the system is lost and the original system disintegrates; I call the interactions that trigger these structural changes in a system *destructive interactions*.

The general result of this dynamics of structural changes in structure-determined systems is that when several structure-determined systems interact with each other recurrently (each being part of the medium of the others), reciprocally triggering in each other successions of structural changes, their recurrent interactions become recursive, they undergo congruent structural changes, and spontaneously constitute a whole that operates as a totality in a different domain than any of them. As this happens, the several systems that constitute the whole that emerges in this way undergo together a coherent history of congruent structural changes with conservation of their individual organizations until all or only some of them disintegrate or separate. I call this dynamics of congruent structural changes in a group of systems that operate in recurrent recursive interactions, as well as the condition of structural congruence between them that arises in this way, *structural coupling*.

Relations and Interactions

Simple entities relate and interact only through the operation of their properties as wholes in a domain defined by these properties. Simple entities exist only in the domain of their operation as wholes. The case of composite entities is different. Composite entities relate and interact as wholes through the properties that arise in them in their distinction as wholes, but as the observer decomposes them into their components, they also appear relating and interacting through the properties of their components. Composite unities exist, then, in two domains: 1) in the domain in which they operate as simple unities through the operation of their properties as totalities; and 2) in the domain of operation of the properties of their components as they are decomposed and operate as composite entities. In these circumstances, the observer who is aware of the conditions of constitution of a composite entity is also aware that this kind of entity interacts through the operation of the properties of its components even when it operates as a totality. Moreover, such an observer may also be aware that although the properties of a composite unity as it operates as a whole result from its composition, they take place in a different operational domain than the domain in which its components operate. This is what scientists and philosophers implicitly refer to when speaking of emergent properties, but I do not like that expression because it obscures the fact that systems exist as composite in two non-intersecting operational (phenomenal) domains.

The composition of a system occurs as a spontaneous process (even if there is a design) in which the system appears arising from a structural background that has entirely different features from those that are present in the new domain of relations and interactions encountered by the system once it has arisen. Indeed, the experience of the observer is that a composite unity arises from what he or she may call a background of chaos or nothingness, as he or she cannot deduce from the properties of the newly arisen whole the properties and characteristics of the elements of the domain from which it appeared. And this is so because the newly arising composite unity exists as a totality or simple unity in a domain of interactions and relations that do not intersect with the domain of interactions and relations from which it arose. The observer can use the operation of the whole to characterize the background of chaos from which it arose because it interacts as such through the operation of the properties of its components, and the observer can see a generative relation between the two domains of existence of the composite unity.

Structural Intersections

As the organization of a system is realized in its structure and does not exist independently by itself, several different organizations can be realized through the same structural elements as these participate in the realization of several organizations. As a result, several systems can intersect structurally in a single bodyhood while remaining independent in their operation as totalities in different operational domains because their organizations do not intersect. An organization exists only as long as the configuration of relations that defines it is conserved, regardless of what happens with the structure that realizes it. As a consequence, structurally intersecting systems remain in structural intersection as long as their respective organizations are conserved through the flow of the structural changes occurring in their shared bodyhood. Moreover, as a further result of this condition, when two or more systems are in structural intersection, even though they conserve their independent identities in their different domains of existence, the structural changes that occur in one of them in the flow of its interactions as a whole may result in changes in the structural realization of some of the others with the consequent changes in their manner of realization. Thus, depending of which is the case, an observer may see that the intersecting systems remain unchanged, that some change the particular features of their realization, that some disintegrate, or that all of them disintegrate. In other words, the members of any number of systems in structural intersection will exist as independent wholes in their different domains of operation if their respective organizations are conserved in the flow of the structural changes undergone by the elements or components that they have in common.

Structural Determinism & Structural Intersections 169

Structural intersection is frequent in systems in general, but it is the norm among living systems where each living system usually realizes several intersecting identities at the same time. Thus, for example, the entities dog, mammal, and vertebrate coexist in structural intersection in a particular living system as long as the structural realization of this entails the conservation of their respective organizations; and, of course, this will occur as well only as long as the structural realization of the intersecting entities entails the conservation of the organization of the living system in which they intersect. I call the basic organization that is conserved through the realization of other organizations that intersect with it in their structural realization the *basic* or *carrying system*. Indeed, whenever a new configurations of relations begins to be conserved in the flow of the recurrent and recursive interactions of a living system in the medium, a new kind of living system arises in intersection with the conservation of the original living system as the basic or carrying system. When that happens, the new kind of living system that arises in that moment lasts as long as the configuration of relations that defines its kind or class identity is conserved. In the evolutionary history of living systems the basic or carrying system has been the autopoietic system.

Structural Coupling

When two or more systems are in recurrent recursive interactions as composite entities (interacting in the domain defined by the properties of their components), they undergo congruent structural changes as a spontaneous result of the systemic conservation of their independent identities in the domain of their recurrent recursive interactions. It is this that I indicate when I say that organism and medium change together congruently while the organism conserves its particular species organization in the realization of its living. And it is also this that I point to when I claim that adaptation, as a dynamic relation of operational congruence between organism and medium, is conserved as an invariant while the organism and the medium undergo spontaneous congruent structural changes through their recursive interactions while the organism remains alive. I have called this particular dynamic relation of operational congruence between living system and medium through recursive interactions that result in congruent structural changes of the organism and the medium, a relation of *structural coupling*.

A system can enter into relations of structural coupling in any domain of recursive interactions in which its components participate as long as it conserves its organization through the structural changes triggered in it by those interactions. Indeed, new relations of structural coupling arise spontaneously in a system when some of its components enter in new dimensions of interactions, and the consequences can be a change of identity in the system or the expansion of the domain of interactions in which it exists without change of identity, depending on whether the organization of the system is lost or conserved.

The dimensions of the relation of structural coupling of a system are the dimensions of the domain of existence of the system. When the components of a system become involved in new dimensions of interactions and the system conserves its organization through those interactions, a new aspect in its history of structural coupling begins for the system, and its domain of conservation of identity changes. In fact, it is the numerous and diverse dimensions of possible interactions in which the components of a system can participate that has made the biosphere a multidimensional network of organisms that operate in reciprocal structural coupling through the conservation of their different individual identities along their interrelated evolutionary histories.

At the same time, since an observer does not at any moment see all the dimensions of structural coupling of a system, systems frequently appear modulated in their operation by unexpected interactions. In general terms, it is the spontaneous openness of any composite entity to recursively become structurally coupled in any domain of possible recurrent interactions as it conserves its identity, which makes the cosmos a network of structurally coupled composite entities that operate as if they were independent systems when examined only in their local relations.

Comments

Structural determinism is not an ontological assumption, it is an operational abstraction of the coherences of our living as observers, and it is as such the fundament of all that we do, including our explaining what kind of systems we are as living systems and how we operate in language. Accordingly, if structural determinism were to fail or did not operate, nothing of what we do as human beings would be possible. Indeed, life would not occur.

Even quantum mechanics as an explanatory system of the particular kind of human experiences that we connote with that expression, arises in an operational domain that entails structural determinism. What occurs in the case of quantum mechanics is that the domain of structural coherences that an observer abstracts from the coherences of his or her experiences that he or she calls quantum phenomena is different from that abstracted by an observer in other experiential domains. Indeed, there arise as many domains of structural determinism, as the observer explains the coherences of his or her experiences, as there are different domains of experiential coherences that observers live. That this should be so, however, is not a problem for scientific explanations because what the observer explains is the experiential coherences that he or she lives with the coherences of his or her experiences, and not an independent reality (see Maturana, 1990). We cannot do science, we cannot explain anything, indeed, there is no language or the possibility of language without structural determinism. Structural determinism as an abstraction of the experiential coherences of the observer in his or her living is the operational fundament of all that we do as observers.

Structural determinism implies that everything occurs spontaneously moment by moment according to the structural coherences present at that moment in the cosmos, or in the part of the cosmos that one may be considering. Structural determinism also implies that for any part of the cosmos only that which is possible according the structural coherences of that part of the cosmos can occur. So whatever we imagine that violates the structural coherences of the part of the cosmos in which it is supposed to occur cannot occur, and whatever we imagine within the structural coherences of that part of the cosmos in which we suppose it may occur, can occur. This is valid for ourselves as observers even when our intended actions occur spontaneously according to the structural coherences of the structural domain in which we realize them. In these circumstance, an assessment of probabilities for the occurrence of a particular event, whatever this may be, only reflects our lack of knowledge of the structural coherences under which it may occur. All that occurs, occurs with the probability of one or, in other words, everything occurs because it cannot but occur.

Chaos is not an exception. Chaos is a dynamic domain of structural coherences that contains asymmetries (non-linear processes) that in its historical development may lead to continuous novelty or to stable singularities that arise in the conservation of some configuration of relations. Composite entities or systems are singularities of this latter kind. Spontaneous organization takes place as the establishment of a dynamic structural singularity that arises and is conserved whenever there are the structural conditions under which it occurs. Molecular autopoiesis as the organization and the realization of the living is one of such singularities. As such, living systems originated and continue to originate in any part of the cosmos in which the structural conditions for their origin prevail. The realization of the living with all its characteristics is a spontaneous process like the formation of snowflakes, and what happens with living systems in their living occurs with the same kind of spontaneity as the falling and packing of snow in a storm. Whenever a new domain of singularities arises, their relations, if they take place, may give rise to a new non-intersecting domain of structural coherences with asymmetries that in its historical flow may in its turn give rise to new singularities, which give rise through their relations and interactions to new non-intersecting structural domains, and so on in an open-ended flow of recursions.

Appendix 3
Systemic versus Genetic Determination

One of our main difficulties in understanding historical phenomena in general, and biological and human phenomena in particular, is our cultural manner of thinking in local, linear causal terms. Thus, our usual form of arguing is "A" causes "B", as if "A" determined "B" by itself. And we are frequently unaware that what we call a causal relation is an abstraction of some local regularity of the structural dynamics of a larger system that we have not distinguished as such in our attempt to understand the situation that we want to explain in local linear terms. In other words, we frequently do not see or are not fully aware of the system with which we are dealing at any instant. As we attend to the linear local relations that constitute the particular situation under our view, we do not grasp the systemic structural coherences to which it belongs.

Causality is an a priori explanatory notion used by the observer to deal with the regularities of the linear flow of his or her experiences. As such, causality is highly appealing in a culture centered on control, like our patriarchal culture, because its application seems to offer endless possibilities for the management and control of human life, including human relations with the biosphere. In contrast to the notion of causality, the notion of structural determinism is not an a priori explanatory notion, but rather an abstraction from the coherences of the operation of the observer in his or her domain of experiences with which he or she connotes the operational coherences of the domain of existence and operation of living beings. Structural determinism, then, is not an explanatory argument but our condition of existence. The notion of structural determinism is not so appealing in a patriarchal culture because its application demands sensitivity to and awareness of the systemic coherences in the domain of living of the observer, and thus leads to cooperation, not to domination and control.

Another aspect of our difficulty in seeing, as well as understanding systems, is that the distinction of a system and the understanding of the flow of its operation as a totality requires the observer to be aware that systems exist in two non-intersecting operational domains. Namely, in the domain of the operation of their components and in the domain in which they operate as totalities. To understand a system requires: 1) seeing it operating as a totality in its domain of existence as a totality; 2) seeing it as a composite entity by seeing its components as they compose it as a network of interconnected processes; and 3) seeing a non-causal generative relation between these two domains that gives origin to the system as a totality in the larger context in which it exists as such. Moreover, because we usually analyze systems in terms of local linear causal relations between their components, we do not easily see and understand the interrelated structural dynamics entailed in the simultaneous origin of a system and its domain of existence, nor do we see the coherent structural changes of the system and its circumstances while the system is conserved.

Because I think that we have to understand systems in their constitution and relational operation in order to understand both humanness now and the origin of humanness in the history of living beings to which they belong, I shall now make some remarks about systems and their operation.

Systems

A system is a network of processes realized by interacting elements that through their preferential interactions and relations establish an operational boundary that separates them as a whole from other elements with which they may also interact. Therefore a system is a totality and operates as a totality in the domain in which it arises as a totality. The elements that participate at any instant in the network of processes that constitutes the system at that instant, are its components. That is, the elements that compose a system are its components only as they participate in the operations that compose it, and when they stop doing so, they stop being components of the system. Therefore, the existence of a system is operational, and a system exists as such only as long as the operational conditions that constitute it prevail. Accordingly, a cell, a family, a political party, an organism, a factory, or a country, exists as a system (totality) only as long as the internal and external dynamic relations that constitute each of them and realize in each of them their particular different extensions are conserved through their operation. And any of the elements, molecules, persons, communities, institutions, and so forth, that constitute these different systems integrate them only as long as they participate in their composition. Any elements with which the components of a system interact that are not components of the system constitute the medium in which the system exists.

In these circumstances, a system arises abruptly and spontaneously in the moment in which an operational boundary is produced that separates a collection of interacting elements that thus become its components from other elements with which these may also interact and which become its medium or domain of existence as a composite unity because they are not its components. A system always appears to an observer as arising from chaos or from nothing, even if afterwards he or she may imagine a generative mechanism or process to explain its origin. This is so because the processes that give origin to a system and the processes in which the system participates as a totality once it is constituted take place in different and necessarily non-intersecting operational domains. The boundaries of a system are operational and arise in the terms just described. Similarly, and according to what I have already said, the components of a system are operational, and any element becomes a component of a system only as it participates in its composition and remains a component only while it does so.

As the observer distinguishes a system, he or she specifies with his or her operation of distinction the conditions that constitute it. So a system is brought forth in the observer's domain of existence by the operation of distinction that he or she performs, and does not exist as an independent entity, although once it is distinguished it can be treated as if it indeed existed by itself. What occurs is that as the observer distinguishes a system, he or she realizes with his or her behavior, in a domain of structural determinism that is thus specified, a set of operations that will result in the appearance of the system whenever the oprations happen in that domain. Moreover, as the observer distinguishes a system, he or she specifies an operational domain in which such a system will arise regardless of whether those operations take place spontaneously or as a consequence of the doings of some other system. I call the set of operations that brings forth a particular system the *operation of distinction*.

A system does not preexist in the domain of existence of the observer prior to the realization of the operation of distinction that will bring it forth. Existence is a cognitive claim, in the same way as reality, and as such it pertains to the domain of operation of the observer as a living system in language. In these circumstances, because language happens in the domain of the observer's doings in the recursive flow of consensual coordinations of consensual coordinations of behaviors, the claim of existence as a cognitive claim gives rise to that which is claimed to exist in the operational concreteness of the structural domain in which this cognitive claim is made. It is because existence is a cognitive claim that a system exists only as an observer claims, or can claim, its existence through actually performing or stipulating the operation of distinction that will bring the system forth in a particular domain of operational coherences of his or her living. What I say then, is that when an observer speaks of existence and of the medium in which the system distinguished exists, he or she refers to the domain of interactions in which it operates and in which it arises with the operation of distinction that brings it forth. Moreover, all this is valid for the existence of the observer, too.

We belong to a culture that operates in terms of considering that we human beings exist immersed in an independent reality. This attitude is what makes us speak as if we human beings were physical entities existing in a physical space, and it is this attitude that leads us to give to the science of physics the epistemological preponderance that it now holds. But the understanding of living systems and of human beings shows that living systems are systemic entities and that cognition is a manner of relating, and not a way of referring to an independent reality that cannot be known or even talked about. This understanding shows that knowing is a manner of living in language doing things together, and that the epistemological grounding of human knowledge is human operation as a living system. Yes, as we explain living systems, for epistemological reasons we need a substratum that makes them possible as living systems. Yet we cannot talk about this substrate, because as we do so we talk not about it but rather about what we do. In these circumstances existence is what we do, and something is there as the conditions of our actual or possible doings are fulfilled. In these circumstances also, the cosmos that we human beings generate in our explanations of our experiences as if it existed independently of our doings, arises in our doings immersed in a substratum that we cannot characterize not even to claim that there is any resemblance between it and the cosmos that we describe and explain. According to me this is not a limitation, it is our condition of existence, and it is our awareness of this that makes us human beings now totally responsible for how we live.

Conservation of Adaptation

In modern evolutionary explanations adaptation, the operational relation of dynamic congruence between a living system and the medium in which it exists, is usually treated as a variable. Following this view, adaptation is usually spoken of as an attribute of an organism (and also by implication as an attribute of systems in general) as if living systems could be more or less adapted to the medium in which they exist. With this manner of thinking, biologists also frequently use the word "adaptation" to refer to the manner of operational congruence with the medium that a living system exhibits in its living (or its operation), and as they do so, they treat the operational congruence between living system and medium as something obtained through the process of adaptation. I think differently. I think that the operational congruence between living system and medium is not a variable because for the living system (as for all systems) this is a condition of existence. That living systems are alive only as long as their relation of operational congruence with the medium is conserved is obviously apparent to all biologists at the moment in which they reflect on what actually happens in the realization of the living of an organism. What occurs is that as one looks at a living system one may think that it would survive better in another environment, and one treats that opinion as a revelation of what happens with the living system. But that reflection reveals only the imagination of the observer. Therefore, what I say is that adaptation as a relation of operational congruence between living system and medium is necessarily an invariant.

In my view, then, a living system lives only as long as its organization and its adaptation are conserved, and all structural changes take place in it around the conservation of both its organization and its adaptation in the continuous flow of its living, or it disintegrates. So both conservation of organization and conservation of adaptation are basic operational conditions of existence for any system. All that has happened and happens in the history of living systems has happened and must happen as a flow of structural changes under the conservation of organization and the conservation of adaptation of the living systems in a process in which living system and medium change together congruently.

Systems as Totalities

A system does not exist as a totality by itself in solitude. A system exists in a medium in recursive interactions that trigger structural changes in it, and it conserves its identity as a system of a particular kind only as long as the organization that defines and constitutes it as a system of that kind is conserved through those recursive interactions. A system can exist only in a medium that triggers in it those recursive structural changes through which its identity and adaptation are conserved. Therefore, the identity of a system is not determined in its components. The identity of the entity that a system is as a totality is constituted in the dynamics of interactions in which it is realized as such through the continuous flow of its structural changes in the conservation of organization and adaptation. At the same time, the actual realization of a system in its recursive interactions in a medium continuously brings forth the medium in which it is realized while the structure of a system and the structure of the medium change together congruently along the flow of their recursive interactions, or the system disintegrates. The notion of *structural coupling* refers to this. I will now summarize and expand on some of what I have said about systems:

1. A system exists in interactions with the elements of a medium that arise together with it as it becomes a system in its cleavage from the medium: system and medium arise together. Prior to this cleavage, the elements that will constitute the system and the medium are not separable because there is neither system nor medium, and any attempt to identify those elements before this arises in its distinction is an operation that can be performed by the observer only after he or she has conceived the system through his or her imagination. A system interacts through the operation of the elements that compose it, and the interactions trigger

in it structural changes that are determined at any moment by its structure at that moment. Moreover, a system remains a system of a particular kind only as long as the organization that defines its class identity is conserved through the structural changes that take place in it, both through its internal dynamics and through those structural changes triggered in it by its interactions in the medium.

2. The medium in which a system exists arises together with the system and all that applies to a system as such, applies as well to the medium as a system. In these circumstances, a system exists in the conservation of its organization through its structural changes while interacting in a medium that changes congruently with it only as long as the changes in the medium make the realization of the system possible. Therefore, a system exists and conserves its identity only while its realization in its recursive interactions with the medium results in the appearance in the medium of those conditions that make possible the conservation of the system—and vice versa. In other words, the conservation of the identity of a system through a continuous structural drift in structural coupling is a systemic phenomenon.

3. The systemic conservation of the identity of a system is a feature of its spontaneous constitution as a structure-determined entity, not the result of a design or a purpose. A system arises spontaneously when the structural conditions that make it possible prevail in the background in which it appears, and is conserved for as long as the dynamic conditions of interaction in the medium that arises with it and make its conservation possible are there. The background in which a system appears is indeed a domain of chaos or nothingness, a domain of structural coherences about which the observer can say nothing before the appearance of the system. Chaos and nothingness are cognitive relations. After the system appears, the background changes its character and becomes knowable through the system itself as this is used as an indicator of the characteristics of the background in which it arose. Accordingly, a system arises and is conserved

only in the systemic structural dynamics that makes its spontaneous appearance possible in the conservation of the organization that constitutes it. I call this process *spontaneous organization* from chaos or nothingness: all systems arise spontaneously from chaos or nothingness, and the chaos or nothingness from which a system arises stops being a chaos or a nothingness and becomes a medium whose structural coherences become visible as they are revealed by the operation of the system and are used by the observer to explain the origin of the system.

4. The systemic conservation of the identity of a system, in its recursive interactions with the medium, opens a space for all those features of the structure of the system, and of the relations of the system with the medium, that are not involved in the conservation of its identity, to change. In general terms, when in a collection of elements some configuration of relations between them begins to be conserved, a space is open for all else to change around what is conserved. In particular, when in the systemic realization of a system some relations begin to be conserved, all else becomes open to change. Similarly, when in the interactions between two or more systems some of their relations begin to be systemically conserved together with the organizations of the systems involved, all else becomes open to change around what is conserved.

Epigenetic Process

The development of a living system, that is the life history of an organism (its ontogeny) occurs in a systemic form as a history of structural changes around the conservation of the manner of living that defines the organism as a living system of a particular kind. In biology this phenomenon is called *epigenesis*, a term that refers to the systemic transformations that an organism undergoes in its life history through the interactions of its initial structure and the medium along the conservation of its living.

Due to the systemic dynamics of the epigenetic process, the initial genetic (DNA) and somatic (cytoplasmic) constitution of an organism do not determine the structural and relational changes that it will undergo along the course of its living. The genetic and somatic initial structure of a living system (its *total initial structure*) determines the domain of the different epigenetic courses that it may follow in its life history as a concrete field of possibilities, but only one of these will be realized in its actual living. In other words, the genetic constitution of a living system does not determine the features that it will develop along its life. Therefore it is inadequate to speak of genetic determination of the characters or features that arise in the life of an organism. It is due to the systemic nature of all biological phenomena that, strictly speaking, there is no genetic determination of the characteristics of an organism as such in its domain of existence. I repeat, the total initial structure with which a living system begins its life only determines the field of possible epigenetic courses that it may follow. The epigenetic course that, in fact, happens in the ontogeny of a living system arises in the actual circumstances of its living as it encounters the medium as if the medium existed as an independent system. However, the place in the medium in which a living system normally begins its living through the reproduction of its progenitors is not just any; it is a particular one that has also arisen in the systemic dynamic history to which the progenitor belongs and in which that kind of living system and its medium have changed together congruently. Human history is not different.

Cellular Epigenesis

The structural dynamics of a single cell—its dynamics of molecular transformations and productions—also occurs as an epigenetic process. That is, the course followed by the molecular changes of a cell along its individual ontogeny arises moment by moment in the interplay between the molecular changes triggered in the cell by its interactions with the medium and those that arise in it in the course of its own internal dynamics. The overall consequence of this process is that the *total genetic constitution* of a cell (that is, the structural and the dynamic configuration of its nuclear DNA, and the structural and dynamic configuration of its cytoplasm) changes along its life history in such a way that when the cell reproduces it does so with a total genetic constitution different from the one that it had at its birth. As a result, the offspring of such a cell may give rise to the realization of a cellular manner of living or ontogenic phenotype different from the parental one. This phenomenon occurs, for example, in the course of the cellular differentiation that takes place during embryonic development when the different cellular lineages (the different types of cells) that compose the organism arise through a shift of the total genetic constitution conserved through reproduction in a manner that involves nuclear DNA and cytoplasm. In this context, two different systemic processes can take place through cellular reproduction in an organism, which will give rise to tissue and cellular differentiation. These are:

1. the systemic conservation in the offspring of the total genetic constitution of the parental cell in an epigenetic manner that conserves the original cellular ontogenic phenotype;

2. an epigenetic change in the structural dynamics of the parental cell that gives rise to a change in the total genetic constitution of the offspring that is henceforth epigenetically conserved in the realization of a new cellular ontogenic phenotype.

The processes of tissue and cell differentiation that take place during embryogenesis are not usually seen or remarked on as processes of displacement of the ontogenic phenotype that is realized and conserved in the epigenetic constitution of different cellular lineages. I think that this is so because of two circumstances: 1) because the attention of the observer is usually oriented nowadays to the molecular processes that seem to secure the regular repetition of the standard molecular and cellular dynamics according to an expected or known norm; and 2) because we usually assume that the reproductive stability of the DNA is due to

Systemic versus Genetic Determination 185

its molecular structure and not to systemic conditions in its synthesis.

The epigenetic change of the total genetic constitution of a cell (in a way that may include its DNA) according to the particularities of its life history is not a phenomenon of inheritance of acquired characters in the terms usually understood as Lamarckian inheritance. Lamarck seems to have proposed that the characteristics that an organism acquired in the course of the life that it happened to live could be directly inherited and appear in the offspring. Such a proposition, of course, is in conflict with our present view that associates inheritance with DNA. Lamarck, of course, could not have thought about heredity as we do now in terms of hereditary molecules, but he was concerned with how the life history of the parents could participate in the life history of their offspring. I think that this theme can be reconsidered. As already stated, I claim, that heredity is a systemic and not a molecular phenomenon, and that it occurs as a systemic reproductive conservation of a manner of living in a process in which both organism and medium participate through the conservation of the organization of the organism and its adaptation to the medium. The DNA plus all the other cellular components determine what epigenetic courses are possible to an organism at the beginning of its life, but the actual epigenetic course that the organism follows in its particular life history arises in a systemic dynamics of recursive interaction with the medium in which it lives. So, a manner of living is conserved through reproduction only if the systemic dynamics that results in the repetition of a particular epigenesis is conserved, and such a conservation is a systemic process which entails the organism and the medium undergoing coherent structural changes. Accordingly, although the ontogenic phenotype that an organism lives is not determined genetically (only by its DNA), it is made possible by its genetic constitution and it can be and is conserved systemically in the organism/medium relation when it is conserved through reproduction. In these circumstances, then, the epigenetic change of the total genetic constitution of a cell or of a multicellular organism during its ontogeny is a phenomenon through which the individual life history of a cell or of an organism has hereditary consequences through systemic processes involved in phenomenon of reproduction.

Lineages

When a manner of living (an ontogenic phenotype) begins to be conserved generation after generation through reproduction, a lineage arises. As I have said, the conservation of a manner of living through reproduction is not genetically determined, even though the genetic constitution of the organism makes such conservation possible. The reproductive conservation of a manner of living is a systemic epigenetic process. The structure of an organism and the structure of the medium change together congruently, and, as a result, when reproduction takes place the new organism is deposited in a place determined by the living of the progenitors. As a result of this process, some of the peculiar features acquired along the life of the progenitors can be systemically repeated in the epigenesis of their offspring, giving rise to the possibility of the establishment of a new lineage.

As the latter happens, an observer sees the reproductive inheritance of the manner of living (ontogenic phenotype) systemically conserved in the lineage as if it were the result of a genetically determined process. But the manner of living systemically inherited is not genetically determined, and heredity is not a genetically determined process. The systemically conserved ontogenic phenotype arises anew in the epigenesis of the new generation through the systemic conservation of the genetic and cytoplasmic structure that makes it possible, and the systemic conservation of the structure of the medium in which it can be realized.

Since the initiation and conservation of a lineage occurs as a systemic process, and the ontogenic phenotype or manner of living conserved in a lineage is not genetically determined, any manner of living that can be systemically conserved from one generation to the next can give rise to a lineage. When this happens, the genetic (DNA) constitution of the members of the new lineage is opened to change in any way that does not interfere with the realization of the manner of living of that lineage and begins to drift in a course constrained by the operational boundaries defined by the epigenetic realization of the systemically conserved ontogenic phenotype. As a result, in the succession of generations of a lineage all genetic changes become co-opted in a trend that facilitates the manner of living (ontogenic phenotype) conserved in the lineage, or the lineage changes, or it comes to an end. What is conserved, in fact, in the constitution of a lineage, is an *ontogenic phenotype/medium* relation.

The history of living systems on earth is the history of the configuration of a biosphere as an immense system of interwoven congruent epigenesis that is continuously arising systemically as a matter of course according to the spontaneous structural coherences of all the systems involved. In this process every living system is part of the medium of the others in a network of recursive interactions in which each living system and its medium change together congruently. Ecological coherences in the present reveal such a history of systemic conservation of coexistence in a field of changing genetic constitutions co-opted by the manners of living that are conserved in a manner that facilitates their occurrence. Or, in other words, ecological coherences in the constitution of a biosphere are a necessary result of the systemic coevolution of living systems on the earth.

From all that I have already said, it is evident that habits and preferences, whether behavioral, developmental, or metabolic become incorporated in the features that define a lineage if they are conserved systemically through reproduction (*systemic reproduction*). It is also evident that such a phenomenon gives evolution both a structural and a temporal plasticity much greater than that expected from mutations and gene recombinations only. It is also evident that all structural and all relational processes involved in the realization of the living of a living system can participate in the process of systemic conservation of an ontogenic phenotype. In these circumstances, a lineage may thus arise through the conservation of habits or preferences, whether relational or organic.

Biologists have frequently spoken of natural selection as if this were a directing pressure or the mechanism that generates differential survival of living systems through progressive adaptation to the medium in their evolutionary history. I think differently. I think that natural selection is the result of the differential survival of the living systems, and not its origin. In fact I maintain that the generative mechanism of evolution in living systems is a spontaneous ontogenic and phylogenic structural drift that results in differential survival.

Appendix 4
Virtual Realities and the Nervous System

One of the central features of our operation as living systems is that we cannot distinguish in the experience between what we call in daily life perception and illusion. This is so because we as living systems are structure-determined systems, and all that happens in us or with us is determined in our structure and in our structural dynamics. Indeed, it is precisely because of this that virtual realities are possible. Here I wish to say a few words about what the experiential indistinguishability between what we call in daily life perception and illusion entails in relation to the nervous system, in relation to our existence as languaging beings, and in relation to virtual realities. This I shall do in a series of short self-contained statements.

1. The nervous system is, both anatomically and physiologically, a closed network of interacting neuronal elements. As such the nervous system operates as a closed network of changing relations of activities between the neuronal elements that compose it in the sense that any change of relations of activity in it leads to further changes in relations of activity in it. Sensors and effectors have a dual character as they operate as neuronal elements and participate in the composition of the nervous system through their structural intersection with some nerve cells. As sensors and effectors they are part of the organism and constitute the surface of encounter between the organism and the medium. So, the organism interacts with the medium through its sensors and effectors, not

through the nervous system. What happens is that in their structural intersection with neuronal elements, sensors and effectors operate as components of the nervous system and participate as such in its closed dynamics of changing relations of activities. The nervous system, therefore, does not encounter the medium, and as it operates as a closed network of changing relations of activity between its neuronal components, it does not have input or output relations with the medium in its operation.

2. The structure of the nervous system is not fixed, and it varies continuously in a network of intercrossing cyclic changes that take place in the structural dynamics of its components through many different cyclic processes with different time constants that result in different kinds of changes: changes in the regulation of the dendritic and axonal branching of the neuronal elements, in the metabolic dynamics, in the ionic channels, in the density of receptors—which in turn result in changes in the effectiveness of the synaptic relations—as well as many other changes of a cyclic nature. As a result of these structural changes, the operation of the nervous system as a closed network of changing relations of activities between its neuronal components is also in continuous cyclic changes of long (some times permanent) and short time constants. In these circumstances, the course followed by the flow of changing relations of activities in the operation of the nervous system as a closed network arises moment by moment, determined by its structure at each moment in the flow of its continuous change.

3. The course followed by the structural changes of the neuronal elements that compose the nervous system is modulated in several ways:

   a) through their own internal structural dynamics;

   b) through structural changes triggered in them as a result of their interactions with other neuronal elements;

c) through structural changes that arise in them as a result of their structural intersection with other cells such as the internal and external sensory elements of the organism; and

d) through structural changes triggered in them by substances secreted by other cells of the same nervous system, cells of the rest of the organism, or that come from the outside of the organism.

A basic consequence of this structural dynamics is that the structure of the nervous system as a closed network of interacting neuronal elements changes continuously through structural changes that arise in its components as a result: 1) of their own operation; 2) of the operation of the physiological dynamics of the organism; and 3) of the interactions of the organism in its domain of existence.

4. The nervous system intersects structurally with the organism at different locations, namely its internal and external sensory and effector surfaces, and does so through some neuronal elements that are components of both the nervous system and the organism. The cellular elements that in this intersection operate as sensors and effectors as components of the sensory and effector surfaces of the organism are elements of interactions of the organism, not of the nervous system. At the same time, those same elements as they operate as neuronal elements are components of the nervous system and not of the sensory and effector surfaces of the organism. As a closed neuronal network the nervous system only operates by generating internal changing relations of activities between its components and does not interact with the medium. As such the nervous system does not operate with representations of the medium or of what happens to the organism in its interactions in the medium. One cannot even say that the closed operation of the nervous system is like dreaming, because dreaming pertains to the manner of being of the organism as a totality. It is the observer who sees the inside and the outside of the organism and who makes the distinction "dreaming", not the operation of the nervous system.

5. Due to the structural intersection of the neuronal elements of the nervous system with the sensory and effector elements of the organisms, the sensors and effectors participate in the structural dynamics of both the organism and the nervous system while the nervous system and the organism stay operationally independent. As a result two things happen. One is that the structural changes that the sensors and effectors of the organism undergo in their encounters with the medium result in structural changes in the neuronal elements with which they intersect. The other is that the structurally changed neuronal elements that intersect with the sensory and effector elements of the organism change their manner of participation in the changing relations of activities of the neuronal network that they integrate. This is valid both for the external and the internal sensory and effector surfaces of the organism.

The general results are also two. One is that the structure of the nervous system changes in a manner contingent to the structural changes triggered in the sensory surfaces of the organism during the flow of its interaction in the medium. The basic result of this is that the dynamics of the nervous system as a closed neuronal network, and the sensory effector correlations that it generates through its intersection with the sensory and effector surfaces of the organism, change in a manner contingent to the flow of the interactions of the organism. Two, the nervous system as a closed neuronal network continues generating an internal dynamics that gives origin to internal and external sensory and effector correlations in the organism proper to its manner of living along its life, or the organism dies. So although the operational domains in which the organism and the nervous system exist do not intersect, and remain independent as such, each modulates what happens in the other through the structural changes to which it gives rise. Finally, this occurs under circumstances in which the sensory and effector surfaces of the organism are operational but not necessarily anatomical in the classic sense.

6. In the structural intersection of the nervous system with the internal and external sensory and effector surfaces of the organism, the changes of activity in the neuronal elements trigger structural changes in the effector and sensory elements of the organism. As a result, the manner of incidence of the organism in its internal and external medium changes too. Nevertheless, the nervous system does not make the organism act on the medium; its activity only triggers structural changes in the sensory and effector surfaces of the organism, giving rise to the sensory effector correlations through the encounters of the latter with the medium. However, as a result of the change in the manner of incidence of the organism on the medium (internal and external) that those structural changes bring about in a manner determined by the structure of the nervous system at every moment, the manner of encountering the medium of the organism changes according to the structural changes that its nervous system undergoes along its internal and external relational living.

7. The nervous system does not operate with representations of the medium, nor does it operate with symbols of the features of the medium, and it does not use in its operation dimensions proper to the description of the medium by the observer. The nervous system operates only as a closed network of changing relations of activities between its component neuronal elements in a continuous flow of changing relations of activity between them. It follows from all this that when the observer sees an organism performing a particular behavior as a dynamic interaction with the medium, the nervous system is only performing a dynamic correlation between the sensory and the effector surfaces of the organism according to its structure at that moment and is not generating any behavior. The behavior that the observer sees as he or she beholds the organism as a totality in a medium arises in the encounter of the organism with the medium in a way that both the organism and the medium participate. So behavior is not something that the organism does, but something that arises in the organism/medium

encounter. This is why I said above that one cannot even say that the closed operation of the nervous system is like dreaming as the notion of dreaming, requires the distinction of inside and outside.

8. Neurons operate as detectors of configurations of activities on their afferent surfaces. This is so because the nerve impulse begins at the origin of the axon (axon hillock) of any neuronal element as a result of a local composition of all the afferent activity from other neuronal elements impinging upon the collector surface of the neuronal element. As a result, not only single neuronal elements, but groups of neuronal elements and groups of groups of neuronal elements also operate as detectors of configurations of activity in the afferent activity impinging upon them. Indeed, the nervous system as a closed network of changing relations of activities between its component neuronal elements only operates as a detector of changing relations of activities in itself. As a consequence, as the activity of the nervous system gives rise to internal and external sensory effector correlations in the organism, it does so according to a closed internal dynamics of recursive changing configurations of relations of activities in itself.

9. The structure of the nervous system changes, through the various processes indicated above, following a course contingent to the course of the internal and external interactions of the organism that it integrates. Moreover, the structure with which any organism begins its individual life history is one that has been established along an evolutionary history in which the organisms of any given lineage and the medium in which they are realized have changed together congruently. As a result of this evolutionary history, the initial structure of the nervous system at the beginning of the life of any organism that has one, is one that gives rise in the organism to the external and internal sensory effector correlations adequate for the realization of the manner of living that defines the lineage.

10. What makes a nervous system a nervous system is not the kind of elements that compose it. A nervous sys-

tem is both its manner of operation as a closed network of changing relations of activity between interacting plastic elements, and a system in structural intersection with the sensory and effector surfaces of a larger system that operates as a totality in a relational space that those very same sensory and effector surfaces contribute to define. Thus, a protozoan such as a paramecium, for example, has a molecular nervous system in the form of a closed network of changing molecular relations in operational intersection with the closed autopoietic molecular system that the paramecium is as a living system, at the sensory and effector surfaces that arise in it as it operates as a totality. Similarly, a mouse has a nervous system composed as a closed network of changing relations of cellular activities in operational intersection at the sensory and effector surfaces that the mouse has in the domain in which it operates as an organism. Indeed, it is because of the manner of operational constitution of a nervous system that it is possible to design an artificial system that will indeed operate as a robot with a nervous system.

11. It is also because the nervous system operates as a closed network of changing relations of activities in intersection with the sensory and effector surfaces of an organism, that all that the nervous system does in relation to the organism, as this operates as a totality in the medium, is to give rise in it to sensory effector correlations that will constitute the organism's behavior as it operates as a totality in dynamic structural coherences with the medium in which it exists in recursive interactions. Therefore, it is because of its manner of operation as a closed network of changing relations of activities in intersection with the organism, and because of its condition of being a structure-determined system, that the nervous system does not and cannot operate distinguishing the features of the medium as if these were independent entities. No doubt that it appears to do so to an observer who sees it generating adequate behavior in its domain of existence. But organisms operate generating adequate behavior in their domain of living as they are alive as

the result of the evolutionary and ontogenic history of structural coupling with the medium to which they belong.

12. In these circumstances, the difference between a robot and a living system resides in the different manner of origin of their operational and structural congruence with the medium in which they exist. Thus, the operational and structural congruence between a robot and the medium in which it exists is the result of an operation of design in which either both the robot and the medium in which it operates have been made to fit dynamically with each other. So a robot and the medium in which it will operate arise congruent through a human act of design. Contrary to this, the operational and structural congruence between a living system and the medium in which it operates, as I have said already on several occasions, is the result of an evolutionary and an ontogenic history in which both the living systems and the medium have changed together congruently in structural coupling.

The main consequence of the manner of operation of the nervous system, according to what I have said, is that as it does not operate with representations of entities that would exist as an external reality, and as it operates as a closed network of changing relations of activities, it only generates sensory effector correlations in the organism that it integrates without acting by itself on an external world. It follows from this that the distinctions between inside and outside, and virtual and non-virtual realities that an observer may make, do not apply to the operation of the nervous system. The distinctions between perception and illusion, or between virtual and non-virtual realities, pertain to the operation of the observer as a languaging being capable of operating in the distinction of the inside and outside of an organism as he or she beholds it as a totality in its interactions with a medium.

Appendix 5
Virtual Realities and Human Existence

The main difficulty that arises for us as observers with the aim of understanding the operation of the nervous system as a closed network of changing relations of activities between its component neuronal elements, has to do with understanding three experiential features of our humanness, namely:

1. the experience of the self;
2. the experience of the other as an independent being; and
3. the experience and understanding of what psychologists and philosophers call inter-subjectivity.

We human beings exist—that is, we are realized as human beings—in conversations. It is not that we use conversations—we are, we exist as a flow of conversations. It is not that language is the home of the Dasein, as Heidegger says—our being occurs in languaging in the flow of our being in conversations. The human being is a dynamic manner of being in language, not a body, not an entity that has an existence that can be imagined independent of language and that can then use language as an instrument for communication.

The *self* is a manner of explaining the experience of operating as a local relational identity as a human being that distinguishes (touches, senses) his or her operation as a body. Existence in language is required for the experience of the self to happen. Similarly, *subjectivity* is not an interior living, it is a manner of connoting how we are or feel in the distinction of the distinction of the self as if this were an entity. Thus, subjectivity exists as a manner of living in the conversation that distinguishes the self.

At the same time, once we distinguish ourselves in languaging, we appear as languaging entities in the domain of distinctions in which we arise as selves, and henceforth we can speak as if we had an existence independent from the operation of distinction that brought us forth, and as if we could use language as an external instrument that is independent of our doings. So we find ourselves operating in unaware self-processes when we ask about ourselves, arise into "thingness" and become selves as discrete entities that obscure our being processes. This description, of course, does not replace the experience of self, nor does it intend to do so; it only describes what happens so that we have the experience we talk about as we talk of the self.

All that we do as human beings is possible precisely because the nervous system operates as a closed network of changing relations of activities between the elements that compose it, and the elements that compose it have plastic structures. What happens is that the different circumstances of interactions of the organism in the medium give rise in its nervous system to two different kinds of interrelated processes, namely:

1. to different changes of relations of activity between the neuronal elements that compose it, and through the internal changes of configurations of relations of activity thus generated to different flows of sensory effector correlations in the organism; and

2. to structural changes in the neuronal components triggered through the changes of activity of the neuronal network in the contingencies of the interactions of the organism.

As a result of these two processes the structure of the nervous system changes in a manner that continues to generate sensory effector correlations in the organism coherent with its manner of interacting in the medium in which it exists. In the case of organisms such as human beings who live in language, the main consequence is that the structural changes of the nervous system are such that they continue to give rise to sensory effector correlations proper to the operation of an organism that exists in language.

Experience of the Other

We human beings live the experience of distinguishing other human beings, and as we attempt to explain such experience, we ascribe a self to each of them in the same terms that we claim for ourselves — that is, as an entity. As we do this, subjectivity arises as the experience in which we distinguish the difference between distinguishing oneself and distinguishing an other self.

In order to account for the harmonization of the coexistence of two or more individual selves, the notion of inter-subjectivity is proposed in psychological and philosophical reflections as an explanatory notion that suggests the possibility that otherwise independent selves may be able to interconnect in ways that transcend their boundaries. In our culture we describe the experience of harmony with others as an expression of some sort of interconnectedness, and we live it as such. However, as we are structure-determined systems, this cannot occur. What happens is that all experiences have the character of something lived that we can talk about only as they arise as distinctions in a conversation, either with oneself or with another. That is, an experience appears in our living only as we distinguish what happens to us or in us, and the experience appears to us with an evocation of what we distinguish in the culture to which we belong.

Since experiences are distinctions that we make of what happens in us or to us as languaging beings, and since all that we live has recursive consequences in our living, nothing that we distinguish as happening to us, be this the experience of self or the experience of inter-subjectivity, is trivial for our living as languaging beings. Furthermore, and since a culture is a closed network of conversations, we necessarily live the consequences of these experiences in our living according to the culture in which we live them, which is where they are features of the world that we live. Thus, for example, sorcery is effective in a culture that accepts sorcery as a feature of its living, and it is lived in the form proper to that culture.

Intersubjectivity

In these circumstances, since the notion of reality is an explanatory notion, and the notion of structural determinism is an abstraction from the coherences of our experience, and since we explain experience rather than an objective independent reality by using the coherences of our experiences to explain our experiences, the other arises as an experience to be explained in terms of the conditions that give rise to him or her in the distinction of an observer. Accordingly, the other is to be explained as an experience of the observer, and not as if the other existed independently of being distinguished by the observer. In these circumstances, the notions of *inter-subjectivity* and *self* become explanatory notions for manners of living that arise as we live the experience of interacting with other human beings in conversations that deal with the easiness or difficulty with which we coordinate our behaviors with each other. A difficulty arises, though, when we do not fully see that the effectiveness of our coordinations of behavior is the simple result of our operation in reciprocal structural coupling, and we insist in accepting the presence of the other as an independent entity as a primary condition—something that we cannot do due to our condition as structure-determined systems.

Virtual Realities

From all that I have said above, it is apparent that for the operation of the nervous system as a closed neuronal network, all that happens in or with it are phenomena (processes) of the same kind—namely, changes of relations of activities in its neuronal components. And this is so for all cases, even when to the observer the organism appears to be realizing different behaviors. This means that waking, mating, eating, breathing, emotioning, reflecting, thinking, or talking are different phenomena only in the relational domain in which the organism operates as a historical whole, and not in the operation of the actual nervous system as a closed neuronal network. No doubt the different relational circumstances that an animal lives involve different neuronal dynamics in the operation of its nervous system. What gives them their different characters is what happens in the relation organism medium and not what happens in the nervous system itself. In these circumstances, it is the normal manner of operating of living systems, as systems that do not distinguish in the experience between perception and illusion, that makes possible what are now called virtual realities.

Virtual realities are illusions — that is, experiences that we call virtual in relation to some other experiences that we call real. According to all that I have said about scientific explanations, the nervous system, and structural determinism, the only experiences that can possibly be called *real* as a reference that permits us to call all others *virtual*, are those that we live in the realization of our biological living in structural coupling with the medium in which we exist.

As humanness arose with language, humanness arose in a historical path open to the possibility of endless generation of virtual realities through the open-ended possibility of recursion in the consensual coordinations of consensual coordinations of behavior of languaging. Moreover, as actual living in language expanded, the possibility of recursions in the inner dynamics of the nervous system expanded too, and with that expanded also the possibility for the recursive generation of more domains of virtual realities. Indeed, virtual realities in the domain of conversations have been with us from the very beginning of our human existence, and our human existence has changed as virtual realities have become non-virtual through their systemic cultural inclusion in the realization of our biological human manner of living.

Yet virtual realities should not by themselves be a source of serious concern. What should call us to reflect, though, if we do have ethical concerns, is what happens to our psychic existence as we manipulate the domains of virtual realities to which we expose one another. No matter whether we are aware or not of what kind of reality we live at any instant, all the realities that we live affect us in the same way in the emotional dimensions of our psychic existence, because there is no virtual emotional life. Indeed, it is precisely because of this that all that we live in our psychic existence is non-virtual. It is the absence of any "virtual" psychic existence that allows virtual realities to become first cultural manners of being, and then eventually, features of our non-virtual living in the realization of our biological living.

Let me expand on this idea. Our nervous system is continuously changing along the flow of our living, and it does so in a manner that is moment by moment contingent on the course of our living, both in our conscious and unconscious, external and internal, relational psychic space. As a result, all that we live, regardless of what kind of living we live, arises in us modulated by the history of our psychic existence regardless of whether this takes place through our living in what an observer might call a *virtual* or a *non-virtual* reality. In these circumstances, and since our structure and the structure of the medium that we bring about systemically in our living change together congruently as we live, our living becomes dependent on the virtual realities that we live as they become systemic factors in the cultural realization of our living. In other words, as we live them repeatedly, realities that were initially virtual progressively stop being virtual, and as features of our culture they become part of our biological manner of living and, hence, of the non-virtual reality that we live.

The problem with virtual realities, then, if there is any, is not how they occur, or if they occur at all, but whether we do or do not like the psychic manners of existence and the cultural transformations that we generate through them. Virtual realities are never trivial, because we always become transformed as we live them according to the emotioning of the psychic space that they bring about in our living, and this is so regardless of whether we like it or not. If we care about what happens to us and to other human beings with what we do through virtual realities, then it is our responsibility to act accordingly.

Appendix 6
Systemic/Analogical versus Local/Causal Reasoning

Reasoning is operating according to the coherences of language, and occurs according to the regularities of the flow of living together in consensual coordinations of consensual coordinations of behavior that languaging is. Reasoning, then, is operation in language according to the coherences of the realization of living. Or, put in different words and in a different perspective, it is the effectiveness of reasoning in our living as an aspect of our living as languaging beings that permits us to say that the effectiveness of reasoning results from the fact that living systems are components or participant elements of a systemic, structure-determined biosphere and cosmos. Accordingly, the coherence of our operation as living systems is the fundament of our explanation of our operation as living systems: *we human beings as languaging beings use language to explain the coherences of our living with the use of the coherences of our living, and we can do so because language, as our manner of living together as human beings, is our living in consensual coordinations of consensual coordinations of behavior, so that our explanations embody the coherences of the manner of operation of the cosmic components that compose us, and through which we operate as living systems.*

Accordingly, when we give a rational explanation of our existence as human beings it becomes apparent that it is the operational coherence proper to our condition as components of the biosphere and the cosmos as living systems that makes it possible for us to grasp the coherences in our domain of existence as living systems through our living. This grasping of the coherences of living and of the domain of existence in which we live has three basic forms. One occurs in the awareness of the operational coherences that take place in the actual flow of the living of living system as they operate as such; the other two are abstractions of configurations of relations within those coherences that we use as two different forms of reasoning. One of these forms of reasoning arises when we use similarities in configurations of relations that we see occurring between different systems as arguments to claim systemic similarities between them. This form of reasoning is usually called systemic and analogical reasoning. The other form of reasoning arises when we see recurrent configurations of sequential relations and we use them to claim causal relations. This form of reasoning is usually called linear causal reasoning. It is apparent from all that I have said that rationality has a circular character that keeps us enclosed in the coherences of our living, which is in fact the source of its operational effectiveness.

Now I shall explicitly consider these two forms of reasoning, arguing from the structural and operational coherences of the explanatory world that arises as a result of their application.

Systemic and Analogical Reasoning

The effectiveness of our systemic and analogical reasoning rests on our inclusion and participation in the historical systemic coherences of the biosphere as an evolving system of branching lineages with a common origin. The biosphere is at any instant like a historical wave front of interconnected congruent structural changes between living systems, and between living systems and non-living medium, that began with the origin of living systems and their subsequent conservation through reproduction in structural coupling with each other and the non-living medium. In this historical wave front, the elements composing it (living systems and their non living medium) show at any moment and at any locality configurations of dynamic structural coherences proper to the intersection of many different secondary wave fronts corresponding to different lineages of living systems that originated at different moments in the reproductive conservation of variations of the original lineage.

Thinking is different from reasoning, as it does not occur as a process in language, even though both occur through the operation of the nervous system detecting configurations of relations in itself; the same operation that makes languaging possible. As such, thinking is operationally both analogical and causal. Analogical thinking grasps systemic coherences in different non-intersecting domains, and thus it operates establishing relations between them that stand on systemic similarities. As we reason analogically, as must have been mainly the case in early human history, we do in language precisely what other animals do outside language— namely, we treat as the same all that in which we distinguish the same configuration of relations. That we can reason analogically is basically possible because all that our nervous system does is to respond to configurations of activities, and we live as the same all the situations that trigger in our nervous system the same configuration of activity, regardless of how different those situations may appear to an independent external observer. Moreover, as I have already said, this manner of operating is effective because, due to the historical coherences of the biosphere, a living system normally finds itself in a domain of systemic coherences with other living and non-living entities since otherwise it would have died. It follows from all this that the effectiveness of analogical reasoning has the same grounding. Things or situations that appear to us as similar in different domains of the biosphere or the cosmos are usually similar as a consequence of the historical systemic interconnectedness to which they belong.

The effectiveness of the analogical manner of operational thinking permitted all living systems, our ancestors included, to acquire all the basic fundamental operational systemic knowledge that makes their, and our, manners of living possible.

Linear Causal Reasoning

The effectiveness of our linear causal reasoning stands on the same grounds as that of our analogical systemic reasoning with respect to the structural coherences of the biosphere and the cosmos, but in relation to the operation of the linear local coherences of the biosphere and cosmos and not in relation to analogical similarities. Of course, in the distinction of local coherences the operational thinking is the same as it is in the operational systemic analogical thinking, but applied to local coherences: what is similar is the same. In these circumstances, the fundamental difference between the two manners of reasoning, local causal and systemic analogical, rests on their different domains of effectiveness. Thus, whereas systemic analogical reasoning grasps and reveals systemic coherences in the biosphere and cosmos across non-intersecting domains, linear causal reasoning grasps and reveals local coherences within the domain in which it applies. By grasping local coherences in the biosphere or in the cosmos that show their systemic participation in the operational effectiveness of analogical thinking and reasoning, linear causal thinking and reasoning together constitute the field of the constructive possibilities in which scientific explanations and modern technologies could arise.

The use of systemic analogical and linear causal reasoning entails a double look that attends both to the locality of a processes and to the systemic context in which it occurs. Therefore, the use of both the systemic/analogical and linear/causal manners of reasoning constitutes the only possibility for the full understanding of systems, as it operates in the double look that attends at the same time to the configurations of relations in which a system operates as a whole and to the local linear relations of its components. This is so long as the systemic/analogical thinking is not negated through a cultural orientation to a reductionist thinking that treats local causality as the only valid manner of reasoning. Our cultural reductionist orientation in thinking and reasoning, through the continuous search for control, has interfered with the understanding of systems. Indeed, such manner of thinking restricts the possibility of an open reflection on the relation between the operation of a system as a whole and its constitution as such through the operation of its manner of composition. A reductionist orientation in thinking and reasoning gives more value to constructive effectiveness than to understanding and leads to a view that treats science and technology as manners of knowing that permit us to control nature instead of inviting us to live in harmony with it. Nature is not to be controlled — indeed we control nothing — and when something results according to our design, it is because we have danced with nature instead of opposed it. But what we do is a matter of desire, of motives, not of reason.

Appendix 7
Reality

I think that in our Western cultural tradition public objects and democracy arose together in the agora of the Greek cities as the citizens talked with each other as equals while reflecting about the matters of concern to the community without anybody appropriating them (see Maturana and Verden-Zöller, 1993). This happened in the midst of a patriarchal culture centered on the emotioning of appropriation, control, mistrust, and arrogance. Moreover, I also think that as the public object (as that which cannot be appropriated by anyone because it is a matter open to the considerations of all) and democracy arose in the agora of the Greek cities, Western linear/causal thinking began its unrestricted expansion. Furthermore, I think that the expansion of local/causal thinking was highly potentiated by the use of writing as an instrument that facilitated the possibility of never-ending recursions in language through the easy generation and manipulation of new concrete and abstract public objects in new relational domains.

As Western linear causal thinking expanded in a recursive fashion through writing, a written culture began to replace the ancestral oral one in a manner such that objects progressively replaced actions and local causal thinking replaced systemic analogical reasoning. In this historical process attention on the future consequences of the action replaced attention on its connectedness in the present, and the blind justification of daily actions through causal rational argumentation replaced the awareness of the emotions and motives that guide our doings as the fundament of daily living. Through the continuous expansion of patriarchality, religious doctrines and political philosophies replaced spiritual experiences as the basis for seeing and understanding human existence, and the natural world became more and more an alien realm that had to be dominated and submitted to linear causal control. As a consequence, daily life progressively lost its spiritual presence as the awareness of its cosmic connectedness was lost, desacralized by philosophical, religious, and scientific theories that placed a transcendental object or essence (such as God, truth, reality, matter or energy) at the center of all reflections about humanness, rather than the awareness of the systemic coherences of life. Eventually "Humanity" and "Nature" arose as explanatory notions that were supposed to deal with two permanently opposing entities that existed in a continuous struggle.

Yet even in our patriarchal history, the desire for the understanding of our human condition has led to numerous attempts to recover the integration of causal local and systemic analogical thinking under the form of different esoteric and philosophical theories. These attempts have been devalued by our modern scientific thinking, but the desire to find a cosmic meaning (connectedness) in our human existence has not been eliminated. But now even our scientific thinking has led to recovering the interplay of systemic analogical and local causal reasoning in the understanding of that which we connote in daily life as reality, and through that to the expansion of our understanding of our biological condition as human beings. Through the understanding of what cognition is as a biological phenomenon (Maturana, 1970), we can now see reality as an explanatory notion, and through that explain our human experience with the full awareness that we human beings cannot distinguish in the experience between what we call in our daily life perception and illusion (Maturana, 1990).

At the same time, many scientists in the domain of technology have invented new ways of creating more compelling virtual realities that invite our patriarchal imagination, centered in the desire for control, to see in them open sources of power and wealth. Indeed, the modern talk about progress in our political and commercial patriarchal culture makes all appear possible to us through virtual realities. This attitude alienates us from our sense of participation in a biosphere that includes human beings as intrinsic components, due to the greediness of a desire for unlimited wealth and power, as if these were the ultimate sources of goodness and well-being in human life.

Nevertheless, the very same expansion of the reflective thinking that has opened our desires for power and for domination over everything, and has alienated us from ourselves, opens for us the possibility for the conservation of loving humanness, if we indeed want it. We do not have to do everything that is possible for us to do, we can choose. We do not have to live all the realities that we may create, they are not equally desirable if one has self-respect and social consciousness. Before modern technological developments, what we now call virtual realities would have been called illusions. Now the great expansion of the technology of illusions through the simultaneous involvement of many sensory modalities with full awareness that they are not "real," makes the experience of virtual realities so absorbing that we can live trapped in them, making them our non-virtual abode. Furthermore, as we are trapped in virtual realities, at least temporarily without the possibility of reflecting about their virtuality, referring to them as 'illusion' seems unduly derogatory. And this is precisely the point.

A particular reality that we live as a domain of sensory and effector coherences is virtual only in reference to some other one that is at the same time considered non-virtual. But is it possible to refer to any particular reality as a non-virtual reality? Every domain of reality arises as a domain of experiential coherences lived according to the experiential coherences that define it. Or, in other words, every domain of reality is a domain of sensory effector correlations that is lived in full validity unless it is dismissed as an illusion by comparing it to some other preferred reality that is called "real". In the locality of our actual experience nothing is an illusion, and, as I have already said, illusions, as assessments that devaluate an experience in reference to another that is accepted as real, arise as comparative afterthoughts that intend to dismiss that which in our psychic existence we lived in full validity.

In these circumstances, the only reality that is not virtual is that in which we as human beings live as the kind of living systems that we are, that is human beings who are members of a culture and a biosphere. Namely, our non-virtual reality is the domain of the sensory and effector correlations through which our organic or biological living is systematically realized in the conservation of our living as biological and cultural beings (see also Appendix 4).

But there is more. As I have said above, we can live as many virtual realities as there are domains of multisensory coherent illusions that may be invented, and we can be aware that we are living them. Yet nothing that we live is trivial, regardless of whether we are conscious or not of what we are living. Nor are we always aware of what we live at any instant — even if we know that we are living an illusion; what happens depends on how we live what we live in our unconscious existence. Our conscious and unconscious psychic living is never virtual. We are transformed and become in our bodyhoods according to our psychic existence, and our psychic existence changes according to how our bodyhoods change regardless of whether what we live arises at any moment through virtual or non-virtual realities. This is no doubt well known. Parents know that their children develop in one way or another according to the emotioning that they live, regardless of whether what they live is real or virtual, true or false.

Virtual realities are not trivial for our lives as human beings, because as we live them, they modulate all the dimensions of our living through our psychic existence in them. Moreover, as we just said, our children will become adults of one kind or another according to the psychic space that we adults generate as we bring forth different virtual and non-virtual realities as we live with our children. Loving humanness, *Homo sapiens-amans*, will or will not be conserved through our children according to the psychic existence that they generate for themselves and for their children through the psychic spaces that they in their turn bring forth in their living. But whatever our children do, or whatever happens to and through them, will depend on the psychic existence that they lead with us during their growth.

Appendix 8
Biology of Trust

Trust, of course, is a distinction that an observer makes of the manner of relating of an organism and its circumstances. In biological terms, that which an observer distinguishes as he or she distinguishes trust is the operation of a living system in congruence with the medium in a flow without fear, misgivings, arrogance, or aggression. Biologically, trust is the spontaneous manner of being of any living system when in comfortable congruence with the medium. When this comfortable congruence disappears, another manner of relating comes to the fore, and we distinguish fear, doubt, or aggression, rather than trust. The emotion of mistrust entails tension and systemic blindness, as well as distortions in the domain of the possible relations between the organism and its circumstances.

A butterfly that comes out of the cocoon arises with a structure that entails the operational trust that there is a world ready to satisfy all that it requires to live. Similarly, a baby is born in the operational trust that there is a world ready to satisfy in love and care all that he or she may require for his or her living, and is therefore not helpless. And indeed, if the baby is received in the manner that fulfills that trust, both the baby and the mother (and other members of the family) are in natural wellbeing. Much of human suffering arises through the loss of trust in the spontaneous systemic coherences of the biosphere and the cosmos. We suffer when we are in tension or in the systemic distortions of the relations between us and our circumstances that occur when we live in mistrust. And most of that loss of trust arises in our patriarchal cultural blindness about the systemic coherences to which we belong as natural members of the animal world in the biosphere and cosmos.

For example, in our culture childbirth has lost naturalness through a medical care that is not based in trust of the biological coherences of our animal nature, and has thus become a source of effort and pain for women. Yet, when trust is generated in the woman in labor by the tender and caressing company of other women (biology of love), the effort and pain diminish enormously or disappear, anesthesia is not required, and the birth takes place as an easy, loving, and joyful experience. Moreover, if caring trust is there, and the newborn baby is put on the belly of his or her mother, he or she acts as in full comfort and wellbeing, with the operational and relational knowledge that permits him or her to reach the mother's nipple (if her breast has not been washed, and if she was not given anesthesia during the delivery). The baby *knows* because he or she has at birth a structure adequate to the moment that he or she is living. Birth is not a trauma for a baby just born, unless we culturally make it so.

I think that most, if not all, the physiological and relational difficulties that arise in a child's upbringing in our Western patriarchal culture, are the result of interfering with the biology of love as the child grows as a member of a family, a school, or an adult community. When a child is loved, and he or she must be loved at least by one adult person, he or she exhibits the embodied knowledge of our biological constitution as *Homo sapiens-amans*, and becomes an active basic participant in the recursive systemic conservation of the biology of love.

Our patriarchal culture, in its continuous and insisting penetration into child upbringing through its demands on both mothers and children for competition and success, and through its glorification of violence and aggression, interferes with the biology of love in the mother child/relation and in the child's growth into adulthood. As a result, mistrust, aggression, and arrogance become the main generators of antisocial behavior in modern human life as they totally contradict love, which is the emotion that constitutes social living.

Appendix 9

Symbolization and Reality

Since the nervous system as a closed neuronal network operates only distinguishing configurations of changing relations of activity between its neuronal components, it responds in the same manner whenever a particular configuration of activity recurs in it, regardless of how it arises through the operation of the organism that it integrates in its relational or interactional domain. That is, the nervous system as a closed neuronal network operates in total oblivion of whether the source of the modulation of its configurations of activity is internal or external for the observing observer. As a result of this, the organism in its interactions treats as the same all the relational situations (internal or external) that trigger in its nervous system the same configurations of relations of activity. This condition is, of course, the fundament for what an observer calls errors in the behavior of an organism when he or she sees that it treats as the same situations that for him or her are different.

In us as languaging animals, this manner of operation of the nervous system is the fundament for symbolization. Symbols and symbolization occur in languaging as distinctions of relations of relations in living in recursive consensual coordinations of behavior become elements (that is, operational objects) in the flow of recursive consensual coordinations of behaviors. Animals that do not live in languaging do not deal with objects and do not live in symbolic relations, even when it appears to us as observers that they react to a particular situation as if it were some other.

Symbolization and Reality

Symbolic relations may occasionally appear in the living of animals that do not live in languaging, but only when they enter in occasions of languaging by participating in circumstantial consensual recursion in the flow of their consensual coordinations of behavior with other beings.

Once humanness was established in our ancestors as a manner of daily living in the conservation of living in conversations, it became possible for the flow of their languaging to become part of the medium in which they lived in reciprocal structural coupling. And indeed, this is what must have happened in the biological and cultural evolutionary history of our ancestors as both the nervous system (or better the whole body) and their manner of living together changed in the conservation of their structural coupling to the different relational and interactional domains that arose through the recursiveness of their living in conversations. In this process, all genetic variations that were produced in the course of the generations of the human lineage must have been co-opted, through the systemic reproductive conservation of living in conversations, for the realization of the different manners of living in languaging that arose along with them.

In general terms, if an animal community begins to live in language, as living in language expands and becomes involved in the recursive flow of consensual coordinations of consensual coordinations of behavior, a spontaneous recursive operation with symbols arises and becomes a feature of the daily living in language of the community. In these circumstances, as a result of the continuous recursive coupling of the structural dynamics of the nervous system to the recursive flow of languaging of the organism that it integrates, the nervous system begins to generate sensory-effector correlations in the organism that it integrates proper to the domain of symbolic behavior in which this lives. This happens as a result of the continuous recursive coupling of the structural dynamics of the nervous system with the recursive flow of the languaging organism. Moreover, as this happens, although as a closed neuronal network the nervous system does not operate with symbols, it becomes a recursive generator of virtual realities in the symbolic domain as a feature of the daily living in languaging of the organism with which it intersects. As a domain of "virtual realities" begins to be conserved in the daily living of such a community, those "virtual realities" become a manner of living in a world that is changing and has changed according to that living, and stop being virtual. That is, as virtual realities are incorporated into daily living in a community, virtuality stops being a feature of what is lived, what was virtual stops being virtual, and a new domain of "non-virtual reality" appears.

At the beginning, any new manner of living in a human community is lived by one or a few individuals, but if that new manner of living begins to be systemically conserved in the community generation after generation, a new culture arises, and with its conservation, eventually a new biological lineage and a new kind of being may appear. This has happened many times along the course of human history as a process in which new manners of living the body and its relations have appeared through the conservation of the new networks of conversations (new cultures) realized through those new manners of living the body and its relations. The general result is that as the new manners of living the body and its relations entail the generation of new relational spaces as forms of community living, new individual and community identities appear. In summary, a culture may be conserved as a closed network of conversations for numerous generations until some change in the conversations conserved takes place. If such a change occurs in the symbolic domain as a change in the manner of living the body and its relations by the members of the community, a new space of relations appears, a cultural change takes place, and a new culture may begin that may lead to biological changes both in the somatic and the genetic domains of its members.

In early humanity, life must have been spontaneously pregnant with symbolic meaning prior to any reflection in search of meaning. A cave and a uterus are obviously analogous in shape. A cave, in the distinctions in language, would have been treated as directly equivalent to a uterus, as both gave rise to similar flows of recursive consensual coordinations of behavior as containers of living beings. This may seem a feat of great abstraction for us modern human beings immersed in a world of distant things, complex symbols, and virtual realities, but for our ancestors it must have been an obvious feature of their daily living, much in the same way as it is for children to equate groups of three entities of different relative size with a family composed of a mother, a father, and a child.

Systemic analogical thinking entails two correlated operations. One is seeing a system, any system, as part of the multidimensional coherences of the relational domain in which the living being (in our case human beings) that distinguishes it lives. Doing that creates in the human observer the awareness that all things occur in networks of meaningful relations and interconnections in the flow of living. The other operation takes place in treating similar configurations of relations as the same, as the distinction that we now call analogy. Doing that results in establishing operational equivalencies between processes that take place in otherwise different and nonintersecting domains in the living of the living being that does it. By doing that we as observers create equivalencies of meaning between different aspects of our living and what we see in the relational domain in which we live. That these two operations as they occur spontaneously and outside language are effective in the realization of the living of living systems, is the basis of all reflexive rationality in us as languaging beings. At the same time, the actual effectiveness of these two operations is the operational fundament for the effectiveness of symbolization and understanding in our living as languaging beings..

Understanding occurs when a particular local situation is seen as part of a wider domain of relations, and it requires the participation of both systemic analogical and local causal thinking. Local causal thinking sees sequential coherences and abstracts regularities in such local sequences. Due to its manner of constitution, local causal thinking entails a linear vision and never goes across nonintersecting phenomenal domains, not even when it involves several dimensions. In that sense linear causal thinking is always local in a domain defined by the local linearity that it involves. Systemic analogical thinking is not local, it entails establishing relations between or across non-intersecting phenomenal domains. In the origin of humanness, the most fundamental consequences of the spontaneous interplay of systemic analogical and local thinking as our ancestors began to live in conversations must have been the expansion of the operational understanding of the coherences of living across domains of existence as reflective thinking arose through the recursive involvement of living in language.

Symbolization is an act of the observer that expands the domain of human existence through the establishment of equivalencies that may become further extended in analogical relations that change with the flow of human living. In the act of symbolization the observer makes one thing stand for another, but it is the emotioning involved in what the observer does that determines what happens in the moment of living through the symbols. It is the emotioning that in fact gives a symbol its character as an aspect of human life. Thus, for example, rituals that we treat in our modern cultural emotioning centered in control and domination as revealing symbolic manipulation of transcendental powers, under another emotioning that is centered on trust, rituals constitute symbolic recreations that conserve in us our awareness of our systemic inclusion in the coherences of the biosphere and the cosmos. Systemic and analogical thinking involve abstractions by the observer of regularities in the coherences of his or her experiences, and reveal the coherences of his or her domains of existence as a human being. In systemic and analogical thinking the observer operates in awareness of his or her circumstances, and the systemic and analogical coherences that he or she abstracts from his experiences, are the basis for his or her adequate behavior. In non-languaging animals systemic and analogical thinking also involves living in the systemic regularities of the biosphere and cosmos.

In this expansion of operational understanding through languaging, two forms of thinking appeared; namely, ecological thinking as a manner of seeing the biosphere as a system of coherent relations, and mystical thinking as a manner of seeing the whole of existence as a system of coherent relations. In these circumstances, mystical thinking as mystical understanding must have given sense to human life from very early on as it made every situation of daily life pregnant with cosmic meaning. Similarly, ecological thinking as ecological understanding must have provided the possibility of seeing the unity of the biosphere through grasping the interconnectedness of all living beings in the flow of their existence through the abstraction of their similarities. At the beginning ecological and mystical thinking must have been formally different from what they are for us now; they must have been essentially the same for the living of our ancestors as they connected them with the systemic regularities of the biosphere and cosmos.

In the cultural transformation and diversification that has taken place in the history of humanness, these two dimensions of understanding no doubt have had different destinies in terms of their conservation, change, expansion, reduction, or loss. I think that the reduction or loss of the mystical understanding results in a life lived without or with only a minimum of meaning in the multidimensional interconnectedness of the human life. Since living in a meaningful interconnection with all existence has been central in the conservation of the human manner of living, the loss of such meaningful living leads to a form of human extinction in "empty living." I also think that the reduction or loss of ecological understanding results in a life lived without or with only a minimum of awareness of the unity or interconnectedness in the systemic totality of all living beings. Since the awareness of the interconnection of all living beings in some sort of systemic totality, at least in the domain of the local existence of each human group, has been central in the conservation of the human manner of living through the continuous transformation of the medium that this generates, the loss of such awareness leads to another form of human extinction through ecological disaster. I think that these two forms of extinction have already taken place in many cultural lineages along the history of humanness.

Appendix 10

Dimensions in Love

We human beings live our daily lives speaking as if there were many different kinds, forms, or levels of love. This is apparent in adjectival expressions such as "mother love", "filial love", "aggressive love", "interested love", "innocent love", and so forth, or in therapeutical practices destined to recover the experience of those forms of love. I think, however, that these many different expressions do not denote different forms, kinds, or levels of love as an emotion, but that they in fact connote only different relational dimensions of our living as loving animals. What happens is that we are not usually aware of this situation, because we generally speak in our culture as if we were referring to whatever we name or connote as some sort of independent entity. In these circumstances, I would like to make the following comments in the terms of my claims about emotions.

1. Love is the domain of those relational behaviors through which the other arises as a legitimate other in coexistence with oneself. Thus, there are not different kinds of love; however, love as a domain of relational behaviors entails many relational dimensions, and there are many different configurations of relational behaviors in which love may take place.

2. Love may involve few or many relational dimensions of coexistence according to the relational space in which it takes place. Thus, for example, in the case of the common use of a street, as we operate in mutual respect few dimensions of mutual acceptance are entailed. In friendship, on the contrary, many relational dimensions are involved, and when we fall in love we want to live with the other in all possible

dimensions of mutual acceptance. In the spiritual experience, which is in fact a spontaneous experience of expansion of love, there is an opening to the total acceptance of the cosmos in unity with oneself. What I want to emphasize here is that in all cases in which love occurs the phenomenon is the same; namely, human and non-human animals relate with another in the domain of conscious or unconscious behaviors through which the other, whoever or whatever it may be, arises as a legitimate other in coexistence with oneself.

3. In terms of configurations of relational behaviors, love occurs in all the circumstances of life as the emotion that makes possible the realization of living through the implicit trust in the coherences of the domain of existence in which actual living takes place. Yet, as we use different adjectival expressions to refer to love under different relational circumstances, we frequently confuse the emotion that love is with the different particular forms adopted by the relational behaviors proper to each of those circumstances.

4. Love, as the domain of relational behaviors through which the other arises as a legitimate other in coexistence with oneself, does not distort the relations in terms of what is expected or desired to happen. Love lets it be and is, therefore, "visionary," not blind, and entails seeing (or hearing, touching, smelling, sensing) the other in its full legitimacy. Furthermore, as love is visionary and entails "seeing" it leads to acting accordingly. The presence of purposes, aims, or expectations in a relationship denies love, as these become the center of attention and care. Such purposes, expectations, and aims generate blindness with respect to the participants in the relationship, whoever or whatever these may be. That is, by attending to what one expects the other to do, the other disappears and the relationship does not take place in love, but occurs in use and manipulation.

5. Love is not blind acceptance. Love is seeing, hearing, touching and smelling the other in his, her, or its legitimacy and acting accordingly. If the other is a child in a

mother/child relation, love is the relational behavior through which each arises in its legitimacy in mutual respect and body acceptance. In love the child arises as a child without being denied in the legitimacy of his or her childness, and at the same time the mother arises as a legitimate being as mother in that relationship. If the other happens to be a poisonous spider, love takes place as we behave in a way such that the spider arises in its legitimacy as the kind of animal that it is, and we let it be in its domain of existence in full awareness of it, or destroy it taking full responsibility for the act.

6. A conflict between two persons takes place in love when it is faced through behaviors that do not deny the legitimate existence of the other in coexistence with oneself. In such a case the conflict is lived in mutual respect even when there is a confrontation in violence, because what is denied is the behavior of the other, not its being.

7. As observers we can only make assessments about the emotioning involved in any particular relational situation between living beings. But assessments are not statements of facts, they are distinctions that an observer makes of some relational features apparent to him or her in the circumstances of his or her living at the moment in which the relation is taking place. As such, an assessment reveals the observer in his or her relational dynamics, and not the assessed. No doubt we know in daily life that this is so, as is apparent in the uncertainty that the word assessment entails. Yet once we have made an assessment of the emotioning in the relation in which we are, we live the reality that the emotion that we claim we have seen brings about, and our life follows a path accordingly, regardless of whether or not somebody else may consider our assessment valid.

8. In these circumstances, it is not sincerity that matters in the moment of an interaction between two living systems, human or non-human, but it is the emotional form lived by each of them in it. It is only through what will happen in the course followed by the ongoing life of these two beings that matters of sincerity and hon-

esty may appear and become crucial. We humans must live in love, trusting each other, to be physiologically and psychically healthy. So if there is no sincerity in the "loving" behavior seen in a human relation, and this lack becomes apparent in the course of living so that a retrospective trust is broken, a physiological or psychic breakdown occurs or may occur. Animal relations in general, and of course human relations in particular, both in their physiological and psychic dimension, are recursively built on the implicit trust in the trustfulness of the apparent emotioning that is being lived.

When love comes to an end through loss of trust, suffering arises that can only be cured through the restitution of trust in the reconstruction of the same relational domain in which it was lost. Furthermore, such restitution is possible only through trust in the sincerity of the participants in the relationship as the fundament for the systemic conservation of the thus reconstructed relational coherences in love that they will henceforth live. And this is so because the identity through which a particular human being is realized as such, whatever this may be, is systemic and systemically conserved, not an intrinsic feature of his or her bodyhood. We human beings are biologically loving animals in the sense that our physiological and psychic wellbeing requires that we live in love all our life. But to live as a loving being is a systemic dynamics conserved systemically through living in love in a loving living, and not an intrinsic condition that we may or may not have.

I think that the greatest difficulty in understanding both that emotional dynamics have a fluid character, and that different emotions as different domains of relational behaviors do not necessarily constitute uniform manners of relations, rests on our classificatory attitude. In our Western culture we act as if every distinction that we make should reveal some well-defined independent entity, and we expect that the borders of the entity that we distinguish should be intrinsically neat. With this attitude we do not see that it is the operation of distinction that we perform that specifies the borders of what we distinguish, and we do not realize that the identity of what we distinguish is systemic, so that it exists only as long as the conditions that bring it forth prevail. In the continuous flow of the relational dynamics of living systems, the different emotions that we distinguish have arisen as different manners of relating that have been conserved in the phylogenic history of the organisms involved, but the form of their occurrence is not fixed.

References

Bunnell, P. 1997. An Invitation Concerning Human Speciation. Proceedings: Biology, Language, Cognition and Society - International Symposium on Autopoiesis, Belo Horizonte, Brazil.

Bunnell. P., and N. Sonntag. 2000. Becoming a Sustainable Species. *Reflections: The SoL Journal on Knowledge, Learning and Change* 1 (4): 66-71.

Heidegger, M. 1971. On the Way to Language. Harper and Row, New York, N.Y.

Johanson, D., and E. Maitland. 1981. *Lucy: The beginnings of humankind.* Simon and Schuster. New York, NY

Johanson, D., and J. Shreeve. 1989. *Lucy's child: The discovery of a human ancestor.* Avon Books. New York, NY

Maturana, H. R. 1988. Reality: The search for objectivity or the quest for a compelling argument. *Irish J. of Psychology* 9 (1): 25-82.

Maturana, H. R. 1990. Science and daily life: The ontology of scientific explanations. In W. Krohn and G. Kuppers (eds), *Selforganization: Portrait of a scientific revolution.* Kluwer Academic Publishers, Dordrecht, Boston, London.

Maturana, H. 2000. The nature of the laws of nature. *Systems Research and Behavioral Science* 17: 459-468.

Maturana, H. R., and G. Guiloff. 1980. The search for the intelligence of intelligence. *J. of Social and Biological Structures* (3): 135-148.

Maturana, H. R., and J. Mpodozis. 1992. Origen de las especies por medio de la deriva natural. Publicación Ocacional N° 46/1992 Museo Nacional de Historia Natural, Dirección de Bibliotecas Archivos y museos.

Maturana, H. R., and J. Mpodozis. 2000. The origin of species by means of natural drift. *Revista Chilenade Historia Natural* (73) 2: 261-310.

Maturana, H. R., and F. J. Varela 1988. *The tree of knowledge: The biological roots of human understanding.* Shambhala Boston and London.

Maturana, H. R., and G. Verden-Zöller. 1993. *Liebe und Spiel: Die vergessene Grundlagen des Menschseins.* Carl Auer Verlag.

Nietzche, F. W. 1998. Thus Spake Zarathustra. Trans. T. Common.

Varela, F., Maturana, H. R., Uribe, R. B. 1974. Autopoiesis: The organization of living systems, its characterization and a model. *Biosystems* 5: 187-196.

de Waal, F. 1982. *Chimpanzee politics.* Jonathan Cape, London.

www.ingramcontent.com/pod-product-compliance
Lightning Source LLC
Chambersburg PA
CBHW051052230426
43667CB00013B/2268